Routledge Revivals

Alexandrine Teaching on the Universe

Originally published in 1932, this book is based on a series of lectures delivered in Cambridge in 1931. The views of the universe as held by the great teachers of Ancient Alexandria are discussed: Philo, Clement, Origen, Plotinus and the Gnostics are considered and their outlook compared and contrasted with certain phases of early 20th Century scientific opinion.

Alexandrine Teaching on the Universe

R.B. Tollinton

First published in 1932 by George Allen & Unwin Ltd.

This edition first published in 2024 by Routledge
4 Park Square, Milton Park, Abingdon, Oxon, OX14 4RN

and by Routledge
605 Third Avenue, New York, NY 10158.

Routledge is an imprint of the Taylor & Francis Group, an informa business

© 1932 R.B. Tollinton

The right of R.B.Tollinton to be identified as the author of this work has been asserted by him in accordance with sections 77 and 78 of the Copyright, Designs and Patents Act 1988.

All rights reserved. No part of this book may be reprinted or reproduced or utilised in any form or by any electronic, mechanical, or other means, now known or hereafter invented, including photocopying and recording, or in any information storage or retrieval system, without permission in writing from the publishers.

ISBN 13: 978-1-032-89253-5 (hbk)
ISBN 13: 978-1-003-54197-4 (ebk)
ISBN 13: 978-1-032-89260-3 (pbk)
Book DOI 10.4324/9781003541974

ALEXANDRINE TEACHING ON THE UNIVERSE

FOUR LECTURES
BY
R. B. TOLLINTON
D.D. D.Litt.

LONDON
GEORGE ALLEN & UNWIN LTD
MUSEUM STREET

FIRST PUBLISHED IN 1932

*Printed in Great Britain by
Latimer, Trend & Co., Plymouth*

CONTENTS
PREFACE   p. 7
LECTURE I

TRANSCENDENCE   pp. 9-41
Alexandrine interest in the Universe—Limits of the period to be considered—Association of the teachers in question with Alexandria—Some characteristics of the city—Alexandrine teaching, eclectic, Platonic, abstract—Order of presentation; from the One to the many—The Transcendence of God—This doctrine in Philo—in Clement—Origen's view differs—Transcendence in Plotinus—Motives for this doctrine—It was in some sense a Theodicy—It was also a reaction from polytheism—All Anthropomorphism is ruled out—A possible loss thereby involved.

LECTURE II

MEDIATION   pp. 42-86
Theories as to the origin of the Cosmic Order—God as the First Cause—After the problem of Being arises the problem of Evil—Intermediate agencies—Such Mediation relieves God of responsibility—And also secures divine action within the world-order—The Gnostic schemes; Marcion, Valentinus—Plotinus criticized the Gnostics—The Powers in Philo—Were these Powers persons or attributes?—Clement's doctrine of the Logos—The Logos was Creator, Revealer, Educator—Origen's theory of Eternal Generation—His interest in the manifold activities of the Word—The Demons in Origen—Plotinus. Two grades of Mediation, Spirit or Mind, and Soul—Spirit is Being—The nature and activity of Soul—Always these intermediate agencies are in a descending order—The Alexandrines anticipated recent teaching on a "Premundane Fall"—Some points of similarity or contrast between ancient and modern views.

LECTURE III
THE UNIVERSE *pp.* 87-132
Earlier teaching on the Universe—The Book of Genesis—Plato's *Timaeus*—Stoic theories—In Alexandrine teaching the universe was not self-existent—Creation *ex nihilo*—Emanation—Was matter eternal? —The astronomical scheme—The heavenly bodies as living creatures—The unity of the cosmic order—The spheres as "many mansions"—Plotinus on the revolution of the heavens—The planetary orbits—Astrology—The nature of Matter—Relation of matter to evil—The universe regulated by Providence—How the problems involved were met—The Alexandrines allowed but undervalued the Beauty of the material world—Contrast our increased interest in physical nature—Also our greater recognition of change and process in the universe—But we share their belief in a reality beyond the world we see.

LECTURE IV
MAN *pp.* 133-181
Man's place in the Universe—The body—Origin of the soul—Pre-existence—Little emphasis on heredity—The soul descends—Restricted interest in this present life—Original man—Reason in man—Ecstasy—A relatively low estimate of Faith—Human Freedom—Necessity, Grace, Salvation in relation to freedom—The Alexandrine estimate of man aristocratic—Depreciation of Woman—Types of excellence—The Statesman in Philo—Clement's Gnostic—Origen's ideal Teacher—Immortality—It was not conditional—Personality will be retained—The Resurrection in Origen—The rise and fall of souls in many worlds—The end as the beginning—Man's affinity with the universe—A difference of emphasis, then and now—The future hope, for the individual or for the race?—A dramatic element in ancient cosmology—Our greater sense of limitation—Yet the present estimate gives grounds of hope.
INDEX *p.* 183

PREFACE

THE four Lectures now published were delivered at Newnham College, Cambridge, in August, 1931, and formed part of the scheme of the Vacation Term for Biblical Study. Their subject was chosen by the Committee, no doubt with our present interest in problems of the universe in view. The Lectures are published in their original form, without addition or alteration.

The absence of references may call for a word of explanation. It would have been easy to enlarge the book by many notes and much "documentation". Such elaboration in so slight a sketch of a large subject would have been out of proportion. And no half measure seemed appropriate. I have therefore given no references. Readers who wish to devote fuller study to Alexandrine teaching will find abundant information as to sources in many larger works. I will only add that to the best of my belief I have attributed no statement and no opinion to any writer, ancient or modern, without evidence and authority. My large indebtedness to many masters past and present will be too plain to need more than grateful acknowledgment.

R. B. TOLLINTON.

TENDRING RECTORY, ESSEX.
Christmas, 1931.

LECTURE I

TRANSCENDENCE

We are to consider in these four lectures the manner in which certain ancient teachers interpreted the world. We are to think over again the ideas they held as to the origin of the universe, as to the spiritual agencies at work within it, as to its visible and material features, as to the distinctive characteristics of human nature, of man who is at once its critic and its child. Views of the universe have become in our own later day a subject of absorbing interest. New factors, new influences, a new recognition of values have brought profound change into the interpretation of cosmic reality, as this is understood or guessed by the minds best qualified to speak of it. This present interest in our "mysterious universe" renders timely and appropriate the selection of the particular subject of these lectures. Many centuries before our time, in the learned circles of a wonderful city, men were greatly interested in the stars, in the elements, in the cosmic process, in time and space, in the relations of the spiritual to the material, in the possibilities of the ages yet to be and in the perennial riddle of the future of the human soul. If they had no Evolution as we understand it, if they had not heard of Relativity, if their Inductive Science was limited in its range and comparatively slight in its influence, still the direction of their interest was the same, they were as frank and as free in their thinking as are our own masters, their love of truth and of knowledge for their own sake was as pure and as disinterested as in any laboratory or observatory of the modern world. Something of interest then may be found in considering how these men of Alexandria interpreted their world.

Plainly we must limit our subject. From the time when Ptolemy Soter (B.C. 305-285) founded the Museum until nearly a thousand years later (640 A.D.) the Arabs brought the city to destruction, teachers of various types had delivered lectures and written books in Alexandria and expressed with little hesitation their views upon the universe. For the most part this long succession of masters, some eminent, some obscure, must be left outside the range of our consideration. We will not go behind the date of the Book of Wisdom, which may belong to the first century B.C., and we will stop safely short of the Arian controversy, closing our period before the birth of Athanasius, while the third Christian century had still a quarter of its course to run. Within this period are found the names of Philo, of Clement, of Origen, of Plotinus, of Valentinus and other Gnostics. These afford us abundant material, if indeed there is not something of impertinence in speaking within so short a compass of men so eminent, upon whose philosophies and religion so many important volumes have been written. Plainly it will not be our aim to attempt any summary of the whole teaching of these masters, but only on the various questions we select to ascertain what was their standpoint and, in particular, to see how far they were agreed in holding any common view.

The actual connection of these teachers with the city of Alexandria varied considerably. Philo was born there and lived in the city all his life. Clement came to Alexandria in middle life, after seeking truth in many other centres of philosophy and learning, and may have spent twenty years in the city as student and teacher in the Catechetical School, before he was compelled to leave by the persecution of 202-3 A.D. Origen lived in Alexandria till he was about forty years old, when he moved away to Cæsarea, after a difference with Demetrius his Bishop. Plotinus, an Egyptian, whose birthplace is not more exactly known, studied in Alexandria under Ammonius Saccas for eleven years and left the city at the age of thirty-nine to teach on his own account in Rome. Among the Gnostics Basilides and Valentinus both taught in Alexandria, though the latter also was mainly active in the capital.

It would be interesting to spend time over the environment in which these men discharged their task. Few cities of the old world possess a greater attraction for us than Alexandria. Its mixed population, Egyptian, Jewish, Greek, rose to something like a million. Round the royal palaces lingered memories of the Ptolemies, not least of Cleopatra, the last of the dynasty. Temples of the gods, including the vast Serapeum, of which perhaps one solitary column remains, were numerous and beautiful. Crowded audiences filled the places of entertainment and sometimes also the lecture rooms. The two famous libraries were everywhere well known and books were made as well as read in Alexandria. The body of Alexander the Great rested appropriately in his own city. The stream of visitors was constant, students, traders, lecturers, shipowners, Roman officials, courtezans. Every night the blaze from the Pharos lighthouse sent its guiding, warning, radiance over the Mediterranean. Every springtime the convoy of cornships set sail from the Great Harbour for Dicæarchia, laden with corn for the daily bread of the populace of Rome. The people were passionate and excitable, going mad over horseraces and losing all control under the influence of music.

TRANSCENDENCE

They were witty, too, and notorious for their nicknames, ready under little provocation for violence in the streets, as Jews and Christians had occasion to know too well. Pleasure and business, money and religion, luxury and learning, east and west, all met in Alexandria. But the city had name and fame and charm, and fully justified its reputation. Those who visited it were enthusiastic in its praise, as Strabo and Dio Chrysostom make clear.

Little of all this colour and activity emerges in the pages of the severe thinkers with whose views on the great problems we are to be occupied. They were men of the study and of the library, knowing little of the ways of the market place and indifferent to the interests of the crowd. Philo was reluctant to be drawn into politics. A visit from Cæsar, an exciting horse-race, a good harvest, probably concerned Origen as little as the sack of Syracuse had disturbed Archimedes intent upon his problems. Clement is the most human of this company, for he remembers a good story and writes of luxuries as if he had sometimes enjoyed them. But Plotinus was ashamed of even possessing a body. It is only now and again that we recognize that after all these men of abstract thought did sometimes share the common human experiences, as when, for example, Clement speaks of the doubt and hesitation which fall upon the mind when in some great library we contemplate the jumble of discordant philosophies which its shelves contain, or when Origen remarks that for one reason or another the human body is never at its best at sea, and we wonder if he was a bad sailor. Or again there is the record that Philo's wife never wore golden ornaments, for the devoted woman held that the virtues of her husband were the true adornment of his wife. Such incidental references have their interest. But we must stay no longer among these minor matters; our subject is Alexandrine views of the universe.

What are the distinctive qualities of the Alexandrine standpoint? what do we mean when we describe views as "Alexandrine"? Clearly the reference is not merely local. For all possible opinions were taught at some time by some one in Alexandria and the teachers who were most intimately Alexandrine in their outlook often moved away from Egypt and taught for the greater part of their career elsewhere. Perhaps three main characteristics may be discerned in the philosophical position of the teachers with whom we are to be concerned. Their standpoint in the main was eclectic, Platonic, abstract.

Alexandria was eclectic for many reasons. Its geographical position tended to give this character to its thought. Just as the exported goods of all lands arrived continually in its harbours and made Alexandria the greatest trading centre of the world, so was it with the commerce of the mind. Teachers of all opinions and from all places of learning made their home here and then left to diffuse what they had learned elsewhere. The missionary cynic, the indifferent sceptic, the doctor interested in religion, all met in Alexandria and reconciled their views with admirable elasticity. The ancient creed of Egypt could be Hellenized. Moses could be interpreted in a manner tolerable to learned Greeks. Eastern teaching found its way through this channel to the west. The Jews had been settled in Egypt since the time of Jeremiah, and the Christians after them were not slow to discover the abundant opportunities of this hospitable meeting place. Amid all this interchange of ideas schools of thought lost their rigidity and sharp definition. Plato could even be reconciled with Aristotle; the worship of Serapis with the worship of Christ. The tradition of the place too was wholly favourable to such eclecticism, for the Ptolemies had welcomed well-known teachers of many schools and, after the manner of patrons of learning, had cared more for the repute and the distinction of the professors they appointed than for the exact character of their teaching. Moreover, the period with which we are to deal was not creative. Christianity was the one new factor, and even Christianity had its preparation and antecedents. The age was assimilative, tolerant, reconciliatory. It had no ambitious genius for constructive and original work, but it loved to incorporate in some fresh setting elements always various and sometimes incongruous as well. So came Christian Platonism and the Judæo-Alexandrine philosophy, oriental elements in the Gnostics and perhaps in Neoplatonism too. Ideas were fused and elements of thought amalgamated. Books of extracts, "Florilegia" as they were called, had a vogue and popularity. Clement is the most eclectic of these eclectics, and has summed up this feature of the time in his two significant sayings, one, that many streams flow into the one river of truth; the other, that the bee gets her honey from every kind of flower in which she can discover it.

In the period under our consideration Plato's influence was dominant in philosophic circles in Alexandria. Yet this had by no means always been the case. For Aristotle had been Alexander's tutor and had exerted a lasting influence over the mind and character of his pupil. It was therefore only natural that in Alexander's city the earlier tone of philosophic thought should be in the main Aristotelian. Demetrius of Phalerum, who came into the city on the invitation of Ptolemy Soter and assisted him in the foundation of the Museum and its library, was a member of the Peripatetic school. Under the same Ptolemy we find Euclid in Alexandria and, hardly less important, Herophilus, the first great master of anatomy and surgery. Indeed through all its earlier stages the school of Alexandria was predominantly mathematical and medical. Its literary achievement was also considerable, at least in extent, and more especially in the domain of criticism. But in philosophy the Museum produced little important work while the Ptolemies ruled. Interest was centred in science, experiment, invention, geography, in the text of Homer and in the movement of the heavenly bodies. The surgeons were not idealists, and the great sceptic, Sextus Empiricus, found Alexandria a sufficiently congenial environment even in the period we have under consideration. But in the first century B.C. there was a marked growth of Platonism. We cannot connect this change in intellectual orientation with any notable names, but the atmosphere is plainly perceptible in Philo and perhaps even in the Book of Wisdom. The Christians were not slow to discern an ally in Plato, and both Clement and Origen were greatly indebted to this tradition, sometimes even acknowledging their obligation. When we come to the Neoplatonists the authority of Plato is greater still. Plotinus is a sufficiently independent thinker, yet even with Plotinus Plato is the master, and a passage cited, for example, from the *Timaeus* is always treated as having authority; what the master said must be accepted and explored rather than criticized. So even in Alexandria, the home of science, experiment and concrete facts, differing much in mentality from the tradition of ancient Athens, there arose this succession of teachers who in various methods and degrees were followers in Plato's way. They too were idealists. They too refused to find satisfaction in the world of sight and sense. They too believed in human freedom. They too believed that in the wider view, but only so, it might be asserted that the universe was good.

Moreover, in close accordance with this regard for Plato, the views of the universe we are to consider are characterized by marked abstraction. A great deal is left out of account. Interest and attention are limited and restrained. Even when observation is possible, as in medicine or astronomy, general principles are accepted from tradition and on authority without the support of concrete evidence or anything corresponding to the inductive basis of science as we know it. This emancipation from particulars left speculation free, and sometimes, especially among the Gnostics, excessive advantage was taken of this liberty. It was one of the perils of allegory that you could escape from statements of fact into a world of unrestrained interpretation, in which the imagination could disport itself without control. The historian rarely appeared in Alexandria. Appian had few predecessors or successors in his native city. And the tendency to ignore events and to live and move among ideas and principles that tradition had handed down is constantly evident. The colour and variety of the Gospels have little interest for some of their interpreters, who are more concerned with hidden and suggested doctrines than with facts. Philo's real interest in the fortunes of his people is not historic in character, and this applies with even greater force to Origen, who sees in Joshua only a type, and for whom events and persons tend always to fade out of their actual environment into ideas and spiritual laws and items of doctrine. For the most part it is in the world of mind and spirit that we are invited to learn and hear. The world of concrete actuality is not for the present our concern. God has no need, says Plotinus, of the virtues of the citizen, and we may likewise withdraw from the particulars of life and let our mind move, untrammelled, among the higher verities. It is a rare atmosphere, sometimes difficult for the human mind to breathe, but it is pure and clear and we are above the mists, and the voices of the lower world are faint or even inaudible. No doubt by such abstraction we lose as well as gain. But it seems admitted that such retirement and restriction are necessary for the mathematician if he is to do his proper work without disturbing influences. Perhaps other approaches to truth and vision demand a like withdrawal. The teachers we are to consider never question the value and justification of their method.

In an attempt to understand what the Alexandrines thought of the universe we must as a preliminary determine from which end of the scale of being our presentation shall begin. We must take our subjects in an ascending or a descending order, and here a contrast arises between their method and our own. For to us it would be natural to begin with the physical world. Starting with such items as the nature of the atom, with force and matter, with the constituent elements into which we may analyse the material world, our account would naturally rise from physics to biology, then to the domain of consciousness and thought, and so, higher still, to the facts of moral and æsthetic experience, till later on there was left to philosophy the office of presenting the complex whole in a single synthesis and to theology the crowning task of discerning God in the universe and beyond it, of conducting our enquiry to its final term in a First Cause for which no ulterior cause or reason could be given. So should we ascend from the immediate to the most remote. Our scheme would follow the direction of inductive process. We should advance from the many to the one. And whatever unanswered questions modern science may have left upon our hands, there would probably be a consensus that our most assured certainties were to be found at the lower end of the scale, in the material world, with which our enquiry had found it natural to begin.

It was otherwise with Alexandria, or at least with those of its representatives with whom we are to deal. Certainty lay with pure being. The original was always more assured than the derivative. "Nothing sense can tell us has reality," says Origen. The opening words of the Book of Genesis: "In the beginning God," have their corresponding principle in large areas of the philosophy of Greece, so that the phases of being are most naturally represented in their downward process. We descend from the one to the many. We trace the cosmic procession most naturally in its own order from the absolute to the related, from what exists on its own account to that which is for ever liable to contingency, interaction, external influence, outward change and internal failure. In this lower domain, as Plato taught in the *Timaeus*, we have only probability and tradition to guide us. We shall best represent the thought of his successors if we follow its stages from the original reality and begin with their theology, with their convictions as to the nature of God.

Their fundamental conception, largely qualified, by no means consistently maintained, as we shall have frequent occasion to notice in these lectures, was that of the Divine Transcendence. God is above, beyond, away, ontologically remote. They are led more and more to separate God from the world, to form a chasm between the uncreated and creation, over which they then proceed to construct a connecting bridge. This impulse, indeed we might say this obligation, to relegate the Deity to an uncontaminated isolation, is seen in all the teachers of this way; it is perhaps least prominent in Origen; it is certainly most definitely asserted in Plotinus. We shall note its phases in Philo and those who followed him one by one.

Philo was a discursive and prolific writer; he was also a lecturer, and no lecturer can be wholly uninfluenced by the knowledge of what his audience will expect him to say. It is thus no matter for surprise that he has not brought his thoughts on

TRANSCENDENCE

the divine nature into any severely consistent scheme. No teacher who accepted Moses and Plato as of equal authority could indeed have done so. His God is remote and yet near at hand, as indeed Philo was quite ready to admit. But the thought of God's Transcendence is dominant and finds frequent expression. A whole series of negations excludes the divine being from the domain of human experience. There is no change in God. He has no needs. He is liable to no external influence and to no emotional reaction, all which and more is involved in the frequent statement that God is devoid of πάθος, a word for which we have no one equivalent term; "affection" is the best. Philo's countrymen would allow no image or representation of God in their temple, and language was as inadequate as sculpture to express his being, so that silent worship becomes man's proper attitude towards the unapproachable majesty. Not only is evil unattributable to God, but even the beneficent discipline of punishment must not be assigned to his direct action, so carefully is the Divine Being shut off from all possible contamination that might arise through his association with the shifting imperfections of the world we know. And sometimes this separation is asserted in a still more remarkable degree.

God, says Philo, more than once, is without

quality. He exists as pure being, beyond and above the variegated characteristics which give its greatest interest to human nature. If the term used, ἄποιος, were pressed to its full significance, we should be left with a colourless Absolute; for of a being strictly without qualities could even goodness be asserted? or righteousness? or love? So really we can say nothing about God, save that he is. This assertion is frequent; we can say that he is, not what. It is an act of folly to investigate his nature, for he is beyond our power of examination. Of his existence we may be sure, but there our quest has reached its term. And in one arresting passage Philo says of the statement: "I am thy God"; that it is figuratively only and not strictly true. For the words imply relationship; they bring God within the range of association and affinity. But God is self-contained and beyond all relation. Terms of possession, "thy", "my", "our", are thus inappropriately used of him in the common speech of religion. Jahwe, God of Israel, has indeed faded away into an ultimate of pure existence. Strictly speaking, is anything left of the spiritual content of the twenty-third Psalm? God is; we must say no more.

Now it is abundantly evident that Philo's theology had in reality a great deal more to say about the ways and character of God. How, having separated the Deity, he once again brings God back into contact with his world we shall try to see in the next lecture. For the moment it is sufficient to observe that no son of Israel familiar with the Scriptures of the Old Testament could ever leave God in such remote isolation. And, at whatever cost of consistency, Philo does nothing of the kind, for he says much about providence, and calls the universe the house of God and attributes whatever is good to God in unquestioning gratitude. All this must be recognized. Not the less is it impossible to ignore the deliberate assertion, made with sufficient frequency to guarantee its full intention, as to the transcendental character of the Divine Being. Now a God without qualities is a conception irreconcilable with all that is implied by the Old Testament idea of the "living God". The two strains are there in Philo's thought, and must be left there, unreconciled. Philo was a philosopher and also he was a Jew. For our present purpose we note the extreme position to which, when occasion arises, his philosophy will lead him.

Clement had grown up in a pagan environment, acquiring a wide if somewhat superficial acquaintance with the teaching of philosophy, a possession which he did not abandon but rather valued the more when he became in middle life a convert to Christianity. As a result he is less dominated by the influence of Scripture than either Philo or Origen. He makes abundant use of both Testaments, having clearly his favourite books, notably the Wisdom Literature and the first and fourth Gospels. But he is no biblicist. The written word does not control his thinking, and few teachers have been more catholic in their recognition of truth in whatsoever quarter they might find it. His interests are varied and his habit of mind discursive. His three surviving works form a noble but uncompleted trilogy and it was left to Origen to take up in his *De Principiis* the task in which his predecessor had not achieved finality. In regard to Clement's theology it has been said that his abstract speculation had little influence on his positive view of the divine nature. This is true. Like Philo he really combined elements which a stricter thinker would have recognized as irreconcilable. It is with his abstract doctrines, with his philosophy rather than with his religion, that for the present we are concerned. In extent the passages which contain this teaching are a small proportion of his surviving work. But they are important and their statements are a deliberate expression of his mind.

When Clement tells us that God is one, that God is unbegotten, incorruptible, that he is without form, without needs, above time and space, alone possessed of real being, that he is not, as the Stoics supposed, immanent in matter, and that he is above the particularities which characterize created existence, he is only adding his personal assent to the current teaching of the school. But in a few important passages he seems to go further. He explicity denies, as an intolerable theory, that there is any community of nature between God and man. Only so can he preserve the divine nature from all association with the confusion and ills of human life. As between God and man there must be no sort of ὁμοουσία or "one substance". Ontologically he will have the separation between the divine and the human complete and unimpaired. So again, with the like intention of preserving the idea of God from all risk of contamination, Clement denies that either the sufferings of Christ or the persecution of the martyrs could be said rightly to have occurred by the will of God. He will only admit that God did not prevent them. The distinction, in the case of omnipotence, between willing and not willing to prevent, may seem to us a little finely drawn, but it satisfied Clement and he preserves the divine immunity.

Elsewhere, in a more abstract vein, he says the God of the universe is above every expression, every thought, every conception. God is invisible unspeakable, infinite, unnameable. For when we call God the One, or the Good or Spirit or real Being or Father or God or Creator or Lord, we only use these descriptions by accommodation, seeking to give the mind terms upon which it may base its thinking, but not in reality expressing the divine being as it is. And in a well-known passage Clement explains fully his method of abstraction or analysis. We advance towards contemplation of the divine by stripping off from our conception the physical properties of body; we take away breadth and depth and length. What remains is a point, having position, which we name the monad. If we remove position, the monad alone remains. Elsewhere he goes even further and places the divine essence beyond the one and higher than the monad. Abstraction can go no further. The advance towards the idea of the deity in its ultimate nature is movement into the void. The soul is guided on its upward path of vision but there comes a point beyond which the way is lost and our mental powers are useless. τὰ δ' ἄλλα σιγᾷ. The rest is silence. Clement's abstraction has been described as the deification of zero, hardly distinguishable from a speculative atheism. The divine nature is so emptied of content that there seems to be little left for our faith, our love, or our worship. We have surely here an over-emphasized Platonism, an exaggerated transcendence. But this is only one of the many items which Clement has packed away into his *Stromateis*, "carpet bags", as this curious term has been translated. The separation, isolation, inaccessibility of God are definitely taught. But his religion was stronger than his capacity for systematic construction. We shall have occasion to see that in his assertion of the divine transcendence he has not exhausted his resources of conviction.

Origen's God is less isolated and remote than the God of Clement. There was a well-known passage in the *Timaeus* in which Plato says that "to discover the Maker and Father of the universe is a hard task, and when we have discovered him it is impossible to speak of his nature to all". Both Clement and Origen quote this passage, and both regard it as a saying of their master deserving of admiration. But Origen's acceptance of this teaching is plainly more qualified than Clement's. Celsus had made use of the passage, and Origen thinks Celsus had pressed the implications of the words too far. It is not true that God is wholly unknown and inaccessible. This attitude is characteristic, and what he urges controversially against Celsus represents a conviction elsewhere consistently maintained. Perhaps two influences contributed to this result.

Origen was familiar with the Stoic doctrine of

divine immanence. And while Clement refers to this teaching only to dismiss it, Origen takes quite seriously the theory that the divine nature was corporeal, of a tenuity and rarity far beyond that of ordinary bodies, yet still, in the last resort, a highly refined phase of material substance. Οὐσία, "being", with the Stoics always did mean something material, and Pantænus had been a Stoic before he became head of the Catechetical School. Such a view would also be welcome to the physicians of Alexandria. It was clearly a common opinion, and Origen, definitely rejecting it, still mentions it as a theory for serious consideration. Is the divine corporeal or not? was indeed the first question to be answered in regard to the divine nature, and in more than one passage Origen is at pains to explain that in describing God as Light, Fire, Spirit, nothing of a corporeal character is really implied. Now the serious manner in which Origen deals with this doctrine of an immanent corporeal deity had its influence in predisposing his mind against any absolute transcendence. The very recognition that persons entitled to respect held God to be a rarefied and all-pervading substance must have helped to keep the thought of Origen on this side of any theory which made the divine wholly unapproachable and wholly out of relation. Philosophy was not with Origen the supreme influence. But even within the field of philosophy there were influences to make him unwilling to go so far as his predecessors in the direction of divine transcendence.

Then also Origen was fundamentally Christian, and the God of Christianity is not the divinity of the philosophers. Harnack, as is well known, has had much to say on the secularization and Hellenization of the Christian religion, and this process went on with notable consequences in Alexandria. Origen in this movement was a well-known leader, at once influential and criticized. Yet Harnack himself writes of Origen that, "It is beyond dispute that Origen with all his abstractions represented the deity in a more living or, so to speak, in a more personal way than the Greek philosophers." He speaks of the divine "apathy," but does not shrink from asserting exactly the opposite, for tenderness and compassion are discoverable in the nature of God. Origen was a Christian in his home before he studied Plato, and throughout his career the Christian influence remained at least so far dominant as to prevent the withdrawal of his deity into an inaccessible transcendence.

But with characteristic honesty he admits such views were seriously maintained. It was Origen's manner to set out for consideration, usually with singular fairness, opinions which were not his own. He is fond of alternatives, and one item in his greatness as a teacher is his readiness to let those who sit at his feet select from possible interpretations that which seems to them most true. And if Plato had placed the Idea of the Good "above being", and if later Platonists said the like about God, this is frankly allowed. We have to consider whether God is being or is above being. Is God mind or above mind and being? Origen speaks of the difficulties which gather around the conception of being, and recognizes that it is possible either to describe God as "being" or to speak of him as "beyond being". This presentation of different views is habitual. The doctrine of the entire transcendence of God is held and Origen admits this. But it is not asserted by him, not deliberately maintained, as it was by Clement. Even his favourite quotation: "God shall be all in all", attributes a great and final comprehension to the divine nature rather than the remote and unrelated isolation in which others had enshrined their Absolute, fearing contact and contamination. μὴ καθαρῷ γὰρ καθαροῦ ἐφάπτεσθαι μὴ οὐ θεμιτὸν ᾖ: "to bring what is impure into contact with purity is surely not right". This was their jealous contention. But Origen is not among this company.

The doctrine of Divine Transcendence reaches its extreme term in Plotinus. Like the Christians

Plotinus taught a Trinity, which consisted of the One or the Good, secondly of νοῦς, whether we translate the word by "Mind" or by "Spirit", and thirdly of the Soul. It cannot be said that in this scheme there were "three persons in one God", still less could it be affirmed that in this Trinity "none is afore or after other; none is greater or less than another". Essentially the Trinity of Plotinus is a scheme of succession and of subordination. The original is not mind or spirit but something beyond, above, behind it. So far as we approach it by the understanding, it must be along the *via negativa*, by the denial of all the attributes and predicates which religion has commonly applied to God, till something more unqualified than even pure existence alone remains. The language of Plotinus is arresting in its extreme negations. The One is beyond being, unaffected by all external influence, without desire, without need, without name. It is not life, it is not mind, it is not activity. It is not anything, for there is no particularity in the One, though all particulars have their source in it. We may speak about it; *it* we can never express. We may not describe it in this way or in that. We must not even call it God. It is prior to all number and multiplicity. These negatives seem to culminate in the statement that the One has no will and no self-consciousness. All positive description is denied us, except that we may speak of it as the One and the Good. It is the One as source of all the manifold of being, the Good as the goal to which all tends. For the intelligence it remains a colourless abstraction, a divinity in relation to which the command, "Thou shalt love the Lord thy God with all thy mind", would be wholly inapplicable and meaningless.

For Plotinus, however, the approach was not by way of the intelligence. He is a chief among the Mystics and moved by way of ecstasy into domains where mind and reason failed. Four times in five years, it was said, he experienced this mysterious contact with God. Of the reality of this experience there can be no question. When he speaks of it there comes through his awkward and difficult Greek a note of spiritual actuality, an evidence of intense feeling, an expression of the innermost secrets of the spirit, which leave us only able to admit that this man has been *There*. When you speak or think of God, Plotinus tells us, you must leave all else aside. He alone must remain. You must not seek to bring anything unto him but only watch lest already you have robbed him of something in your thought. Over against all the passages in which Plotinus goes to the extremes of abstraction and transcendence we have to set others in which this mystic experience finds expression. In these we find a warmth and inspiration, a sense of spiritual freedom and exaltation and a reality of communion with higher things which admit no question, in spite of all their marked divergence from what in purely philosophic language he is wont to say of God. In such experience there is, as he says, "a presence higher than understanding". We may find it difficult to reconcile his spiritual history with his intellectual theories, but we can never doubt that both elements are there.

The extreme transcendence which we find in Plotinus's account of God has been variously explained. He was for eleven years the pupil of Ammonius Saccas, but he has told us nothing of the extent to which he was indebted to his master's influence. Nor can we assign much importance to his journey to the east under the Emperor Gordian. He went on military service and was away only a year and probably had little opportunity for enquiry into Persian and Indian philosophies. But he was interested, Porphyry tells us, in eastern thought, and some of his interpreters, especially on the Continent, and Mr. G. R. S. Mead in our own country, have believed his mysticism had an oriental origin and character. Neither Caird nor Inge allow this. And the masters Plotinus expressly acknowledges are Plato and the ancients. He hints at nothing to correspond with the intercourse Apollonius of Tyana had with the Brahmins. He may then best be regarded as the teacher of Hellenic and especially of the Platonic philosophy in its extremest form. Whether, in his assertion of the divine transcendence, in his insistent separation of God from the world, he has not left us with an unresolved dualism is a question to which our next lecture may provide material for answer. A deity without will or consciousness must in any case raise difficulties for theological thought. Plotinus, like Clement and Philo, advises silence in such a presence, not by any means following his own counsel, for even Inge admits that Plotinus has said too much about the One.

What is the motive behind this isolation of the divine? What is it these teachers wish either to avoid or to secure by relegating God to inaccessibility? The very gods of Epicurus, living their blissful lives apart, without care or concern for the affairs of the lower world, are not more cut off and unrelated than this lonely unit, which is the ultimate term of abstract thinking. We shall probably best account for this extreme separation by regarding it as an attempt to save the divine from contamination. The One at any cost must be saved from the many. There must be no contact between God in his real being and the confusions or defections of the world we know. "I will say anything," asserted Basilides, "rather than admit that Providence is evil." This motive in its last results gives us the "Deus Absconditus", so far removed from all characterization that God becomes the equivalent of "Nothing". Such isolation had its earlier forms or anticipations. The Jew, who would admit no image of the divine in his temple and who refused even to utter the incommunicable Name, sought to isolate God in the seclusion of utter moral purity. However much iniquity should abound, he could speak of Jahwe as "of purer eyes than to behold iniquity". "Can'st thou by searching find out God?" "God is in heaven and thou upon earth, therefore let thy words be few." There is a sense in which such reverence is right, when man is concerned with the highest things. But our restraint may be carried to such an extreme as makes all positive assertion in regard to the divine nature impossible. And if the Jew was jealous for God's moral purity, the like motive shewed itself in Platonism in an intellectual form. The world of ideas must be separate from the world of sense. Real being is the object of pure knowledge, so that only after death, removed from the limitations of the body, can the soul know God. In all their transcendentalism the Alexandrines had plainly their forerunners.

A further influence is to be found in the reaction of thoughtful minds from the multiplicity of divinities with which the age was familiar. To say nothing of the deities of Homer, there were the gods of every race around the Mediterranean to crowd the hospitable Pantheon. In Egypt the bull, the crocodile, the cat, were objects of worship. Apotheosis made the most indifferent Cæsar divine, "inter divos receptus". On the Pharos lighthouse the inscription "To the Saviour Gods", if originally intended to denote Castor and Pollux, was often referred to Ptolemy Soter and Berenice. From such multiplicity and vulgarization of the divine severer souls turned with impatience to a loftier quest, and, surrendering much, sought for God in the higher altitudes where at least he was free from risk of ridicule or stain. In effect their work was in the nature of a Theodicy. From all contact with the imperfect, from all responsibility for evil in the world, they preserved their conception of the deity free. From every liability to question or criticism he is left immune. Verily "Thou art a God that hidest thyself".

It is plain that on these principles anything of the nature of Anthropomorphism is wholly inadmissible. And our Platonists are agreed in their warning that we must be careful not to assign human attributes to a nature more than human. To say, in the language of Scripture, that God is angry, or that the Lord repents, that God comes down, and that he walks in gardens, is not in the letter true. Philo and Origen are quite prepared to admit that in such connection there is no justification for the literalists. Their common method is to escape from these difficulties by an abundant use of allegory. The crudest statements of an earlier time are converted into spiritual teaching quite remote from the writer's original intention. The divinity is thus freed from the human limitations which are plainly involved by the narrative.

Up to a point most exegesis of Scripture which is not of the fundamentalist type would allow the principle in question. God is not as a man, and we make use of human terminology in regard to him only by recognized accommodation, without really attributing our limitations to the divine. It may however be well to note in concluding this lecture what is involved by an entire abandonment of all anthropomorphic views.

There was a great fusion of Hellenic and Christian teaching in Alexandria. Nothing was more distinctively Alexandrine than this fusion as we see it in Clement and Origen. But at least in one important item Hellenism in its extreme phases is difficult to reconcile with the Christian religion. For in the philosophic doctrine of God there is no place for anything anthropomorphic. God is not liable to πάθος, while man is constantly so affected. In the One of Plotinus it is difficult to find room for anything like emotion. We must not say God feels. Yet probably the only ground for Christian teaching on the love and fatherhood of God is really anthropomorphic in character. In nature we find power and order and even purpose, but there is no certain evidence for love. In the course of history you may find great moral principles from time to time stand clear in arresting expression, but the God of history is a God of righteousness rather than of love, and has even been charged with generally siding with the big battalions. It is only in distinctively human nature that we find love operating, and there it is the highest of all man's attributes. If we may not take the highest of all our nature's assets, if we may not argue from the highest in man to the nature of the divine, from the derived to its source, then it is difficult to see on what basis of reason we claim the right to speak of the love of God. But to argue from man's nature to God's is anthropomorphism. It is the method of both the Old and New Testaments. "Like as a father pitieth his children"; or "The Lord thy God bare thee as a man doth bear his son"; and again: "If ye then being evil know how to give good gifts unto your children, how much more shall my father which is in heaven." The highest element in human nature is taken to have its counterpart in the divine. The doctrine of the Incarnation would indeed be difficult, if we might not hold a certain natural affinity between the best in man and the character of God. If our thoughts of God are to have meaning and validity they must inevitably be fashioned by our experience. We take the highest experience given to us. Something to account for this, something not essentially alien from this, must exist, we claim, in the divine nature. Let us again admit that such a method of argument is anthropomorphic. I do not know how without it we are to find substantial ground for a belief in the love of God, unless we simply accept this on the absolute authority of Jesus Christ. Equally I do not know how you are to find place for such a divine fatherhood in that transcendent remote and isolated deity which is left us, when the method of abstraction has fulfilled its task even unto the end.

LECTURE II

MEDIATION

We have seen in the previous lecture that the doctrine of the transcendence of God leaves us with an isolated, self-contained, self-sufficient deity, devoid of will, desire, even of consciousness. The question at once arises: Why does such a Being create or originate anything beyond its own perfection? For what aim or purpose does God pass out of his own unbroken quiescence? Why should the One give rise to the manifold? What need of a universe to a divinity which knows no needs? So we are led to the old unanswered riddle: Why God made the world. Our Alexandrine teachers provide no real solution of the problem, but their suggestions, if inconclusive, are worth consideration.

The cause of God's creative action lies, it is often said, in his goodness. This theory, explicitly taught in Plato's *Timaeus*, is found again in Philo and in Clement. Being good God did not grudge the joy of existence to others, and therefore produced the universe. The Creator is essentially beneficent. The Christian fathers are constantly asserting that the world was made by a God who is good, as against the disturbing heresy of Marcion who saw in the universe the handiwork of a Demiurge who might be just (much as we say nature is "fair") but who certainly was not the God of love who had been only revealed in Jesus Christ.

Or again it is from the inherent activity of the divine nature that creation takes its rise. The rest and quiescence of God is not inaction. It is difficult to think of being apart from doing, and even those who placed God above being find it impossible to deny to him all forms of self-expression. Philo goes so far as to say that the order and regulation of the universe are God's concern, necessary to him for occupation. Were the world to pass away Philo's God would be miserable for want of employment. "I hesitate," Philo writes, "to add what it would be impious to say, that death will ensue to God if absolute inactivity falls to his lot." The joy of an artificer in his craft has its counterpart in the delight and interest which his handiwork affords to God.

There is also the idea of generation, fatherhood. This is common to Biblical and Hellenic teaching. Plato could speak of God as the Father of the universe. The Cosmos, a living creature, is God's son. Fatherhood is involved in the Christian Trinity. Even in Plotinus, who in this point has close affinity with Origen, the second existence in the trinitarian scheme is generated from the One. In the teaching of Jesus on the Divine Fatherhood the idea of spiritual affinity and parental care are prominent. In the Alexandrines we have a more ontological type of relationship. Derived existence is their main thought. "That which is perfect always generates." So in Plotinus νοῦς or Spirit may be said to be the offspring of the One.

All these accounts of the relationship between the original and the originated, whether they speak of God's goodness or activity or fatherhood, imply a divine will. Creation was intentional, deliberate. God said: "Let these things be." God willed that the cosmos should be such as he made it. There was purpose, design, intention throughout, so that the analogy of the craftsman and his work in this respect holds good. "Of his own will begat he us, that we should be the firstfruits of his creatures." But sometimes we have a different conception. It is not said that the world originated by accident, or that the aimless flow of atoms resulted in the universe that we know. With such teaching the Alexandrines were wholly at variance. But we find the theory of emanation, procession, of a divine going forth, which comes about from the nature of the divine rather than by an act of will. This view is most clearly expressed in the account Plotinus gives us of the origin of the Neoplatonic Trinity. The One, he says, overflowed, ὑπερερρύη ἐξερρύη. The One is as a spring, from which derives a stream which goes forth without causing any diminution in its source. The One imparts being, without willing or desiring so to do. It is all a matter of nature rather than of intention. Plotinus has denied will to his One, so that such modes of expression are alone left when he attempts to describe in what manner the One is the cause of being. It is a remark of Zeller's that when the philosopher makes use of pictorial language, it is usually because he is not quite sure what he means.

But whether the Original passes beyond itself and causes a universe by will and purpose, or just by virtue of its inherent nature so to do, in either case it is clear that our teachers have not only abandoned their doctrines of entire transcendence, but have even adopted views which are destructive of the extreme element in their teaching. In some way or other they all represent God as the cause. Whatever is a cause is obviously related. A cause that is not related to its results is a cause no longer. All the suggestions they offer as to the origin of the universe have this in common that they involve a discussion of the unknowable, a linking up of the Absolute to particular things. There results inevitably the problem, not only why God made the world, but, if God did make the world, or even since God has made the world, why do we find the world as it is? Admittedly God is perfect. But can a perfect Creator make an imperfect universe? From the problem of being we pass to the problem of evil; πόθεν τὸ κακόν; the question caused the Alexandrines much trouble and concern. For, on the one hand, they are committed to the doctrine of God's absolute goodness; on the other, the universe has its obvious imperfections, both moral and physical.

It cannot be claimed for the Alexandrines, or indeed for any other school of thought, that they have solved the problem of evil. But they relieve God of responsibility for it by their doctrine of intermediate being. What is unworthy of God may not be equally unworthy of his subordinate ministers. Qualities and activities which must not be attributed to the One may be discoverable, without entire sacrifice of the divine goodness, in the many. What God himself by virtue of his own nature must not do is less impermissible in his agents. The theory of course does not in reality protect the divine goodness. *Qui facit per alium facit per se* is not a principle that can be lightly abandoned in theology and retained in law. However many grades of being we interpose between the original cause and the present particular results, at some point the problem must arise: Why this transition from the better to the worse, from the absolute to the related, from the one to the many, from perfection to the imperfect? There is a decline if not a fall, nor will even a large allowance of moral freedom to God's ministers, as to the Satan in the book of Job, entirely protect the original goodness from all question or complaint. Still, the Alexandrine doctrine of mediation did something to abate the crude dualism which would otherwise be inevitable. It made the transition from the ideal to the concrete less difficult and abrupt and, taken in conjunction with such other partial explanations of evil as they knew, provided schemes of being within which both the highest and the lowest items could find inclusion. In the main they found mental rest in the theories they maintained. Origen, for example, critical as he is, and readily as he admits that some other view may be more true than his own, allows the existence of evil without any loss of faith in God.

In another way also this belief in intermediate agencies did them service. We have recognized their tendency to isolate God. The Unapproachable, the Most High, the Existence which we must recognize in silence and for which we can find no name, is very far from average human interest and the common things of life. But they bring God back into all the details, almost as completely as the Stoics did by their theory of immanence, not directly but through subordinate agencies. The Word in Clement, the Soul in Plotinus, the manifold Christ in Origen, are all concerned with the particulars of existence, and through their mediation it may be still claimed that the universe belongs to God. In their actual religious outlook these transcendental teachers come more near than we might expect to the principle of the Lord's saying that no sparrow falls to the ground without your father's care. The remoteness of the Absolute is mitigated by the host of lesser divinities, ranging from guardian Angels to the co-eternal Logos, who have all their several ministries and by whose constant activity it comes that the universe is kept in touch with God. Providence, for example, is of God, though we can hardly say that Providence is God. St. Paul spoke of "thrones, dominions, principalities and powers", all of them divine agencies inferior to the Father, subordinate to the Son, which had their place and office in the intermediate spiritual world. The universe must indeed have seemed strangely full of these powers of good and evil, for there were demons as well as spirits and angels, and even the stars were alive. In this way continuity and succession seem rather than dualism to be characteristic of the Alexandrine universe.

This principle of mediation, which at once secured God from contact with the lower things and yet also provided an upward and downward way between the extremes of being, is common in one form or another to all the teachers with whom we are concerned. We will consider it first as it appears in the Gnostics. They were a numerous and varied company, speculative and imaginative in their outlook, making great claims for their teaching and recognizing little control in the fabrication of their theories. It has been said of them in a German epigram that any idea which is difficult to locate or define may safely be described as Gnostic. But there were great as well as minor minds among them, and we have always to remember that only fragments of their writings are left to us and that we hear of them mainly, as we hear of the Sophists and the Pharisees, through the accounts of their opponents. The orthodox fathers saw in Gnosticism a real danger, and it is true that the Gnostic elimination of the historical element from the Christian religion would have had disastrous consequences. Heresy and orthodoxy were however at one in this that each interposed one or more subordinate agencies between God and the universe.

Marcion had no direct connection with Alexandria, and his type of mind was not essentially Gnostic. He was, however, definitely dualistic, separating the Old Testament from the New and seeing in his creator or demiurge a lesser power, who was the rival rather than the minister of the good God revealed by Jesus Christ. But though Marcion's line of approach was different from that, for example, of Basilides, still for Marcion as for other Gnostics the universe is the work of a creator inferior to the Supreme Deity. The creator of the book of Genesis is not the Father. The distinction is just as sharply drawn as is the distinction sometimes drawn in our own time between Nature and the Spirit. Marcion's teaching was well known in Alexandria, though his affinities with the city were slight. His subordinate creator was, however, a common conception of the time.

Very different from Marcion, more truly Alexandrine and more characteristically Gnostic, was Valentinus, who was in spirit poet as well as philosopher, with as much of the mystic as of the thinker in his nature. He was born in Egypt, and was a student and afterwards taught in Alexandria, but was still in this earlier period of his life a Catholic Christian. Later on he founded his school in Rome and was successful in winning adherents, but he still claimed to be within, not outside, the

Church. Our present interest lies in his scheme of intermediate existences. These are recognized as elements in the teaching of Valentinus himself. The Valentinians, after their master's day, developed much of his doctrine, and by no means all that is termed Valentinian goes back to Valentinus himself. But the highly poetical account of the history of the pre-mundane world which is associated with his name was clearly his own. Tradition, De Faye says, is certainly right in assigning this speculative vision to the master of this school. Its traces survive in some of the few fragments of his own writings that we possess, and his later followers had not sufficient capacity for its invention.

Before the world was, within the Pleroma or habitation of the highest spiritual existences, dwelt the thirty Æons, ordered in three companies of eight and ten and twelve, each group further removed than the last from the original Bythos or Abyss. Bythos was the supreme Deity, sometimes associated with the other æons in the Pleroma, sometimes regarded as apart from them, their source and origin but not one of their number. These æons were male and female, in pairs of combined syzygies. From Abyss and Silence proceed Mind and Truth, from these Word and Life, then Man and Church. These form the Ogdoad or Octave. Further away comes the second group of ten; further still the final twelve, of whom the last æon was Sophia or Achamoth. Filled with an unholy curiosity this youngest æon desired to behold the nature of the primal Father, Bythos, and moved into the higher part of the pleroma in the rash attempt to accomplish her purpose. But her ambition was beyond her powers and Sophia would have dissolved and ceased to exist had not Horos or Boundary rescued her. Out of the pangs of Sophia's frustrated passion, out of her fear and grief and tears, came matter. Later the demiurgos came into being, and out of the matter to which Sophia had given birth the demiurgos made the world. How the Redeemer purified the fallen Sophia and readmitted her within the pleroma, how under the providence of the Supreme Father the last pair of æons, Christ and the Holy Spirit, were born of Mind, are later items in the story of much mystical significance. But we must not stay to consider these in detail. Curiosity led Sophia to her fall, and from her fall resulted the calamity of the world's existence.

Such are the bare outlines of the metaphysical poem of perhaps the greatest of the Gnostics. The colour, the radiance, the delicate embroidery of thought, which may well have marked the original work in its unbroken perfection, have inevitably been lost. Its survival, its freedom from subsequent modification, the variety of the sources from which we learn its character, all point to the attraction it must have exercised on many minds in an imaginative age.

Plotinus had some acquaintance with Gnosticism. Certain of his own followers had come over to Neoplatonism from Gnosticism and had not seen it necessary to abandon their early ideas. Out of consideration for their convictions he criticizes Gnosticism, evidently with the Valentinians especially in view, with some restraint, but several of his objections are sufficiently plain and his arguments in opposing a school of thought not without affinities to his own are of interest.

In the first place he thought the Gnostics had perverted Plato. The similarity between the æons and the Platonic ideas has often been remarked. Both are abstract spiritual forms; though perhaps the æons are more nearly personal and more definitely hypostatized.

But the Gnostics, Plotinus thought, had added to Plato all sorts of novelties. In the myth of Sophia's fall was nothing of real value. Gnostic pessimism in regard to the universe was exaggerated. The Valentinians had too little respect for ancient tradition. Their system was an arbitrary and disordered amalgamation. To which the

Gnostics might have replied that while everyone accepted Plato, everyone also interpreted him, and that interpretation may sometimes be boldly constructive.

A second objection blamed the multiplicity of the Gnostic æons. Plotinus contrasts the restraint of his own trinity with the thirty æons of the pleroma. The Gnostics had needlessly increased the number of intermediate beings, setting up a plurality of spiritual essences, which detracted from the dignity and elevation of mind and spirit, for multiplicity involved degradation. It is a fair criticism that nothing is gained by the interposition of grade after grade of being. The bridging of the distance between the first and the last is rendered no easier by multiplying the stages, and superfluous hypotheses are always an encumbrance. This all holds good if Plotinus was right in treating the scheme of Valentinus as seriously ontological. Such was the character and intention of his own doctrine, but we must not press the poets too hardly in the court of rigid reason. Perhaps the real place for the creation of Valentinus is with the myths of Plato and the parables of the Lord. Truth is embodied in a tale. If the æons were too many, the saints were one day to be more numerous still.

To some extent this answer may hold good with regard to a third criticism urged by Plotinus against the Gnostics; he said they claimed to know but they offered no proofs. Their speculations, he urged in effect, were unfounded and uncontrolled. They bring not evidence but arbitrary assertion. Allow that we must not expect from a poet the same kind of reasoning we demand from the mathematician, there still remains the consideration that all the Gnostics were not poets but sometimes dogmatic and assertive persons convinced of their own spiritual and intellectual superiority, claiming illumination, insusceptible to argument. Against minds of this type Plotinus makes valid criticism. Their claim to authority was without foundation. It remains that Plotinus equally with the Gnostics believed in intermediate spiritual agencies. For both, between God and the universe there had been an interval unbridged. For both, it was out of this common problem of relating the unconnected that their theories of mediation, reasonable or unbalanced, took their rise.

As a second example of mediation we may consider the Powers which play an important part in the theology of Philo. These are heavenly and spiritual entities which share the divine nature and yet are subordinate to the supreme God, acting as his ministers, manifesting his character, accomplishing his purposes. These powers are numerous; "God, being one, has about him an unspeakable number of powers." When, in the book of Genesis God says "Let *us* make man", it is the powers who are addressed. They share with God the task of creation, and when the universe is made it is they who preserve it in operation. That the whole cosmos does not collapse into disorder and confusion is due to the action of these beneficent agencies which sustain all things in their proper place and function. Themselves essentially immaterial they still have capacity to act upon material things. Matter, which in its own nature has neither form nor quality, receives from the action of the powers its characterization and determination, so that all particular objects are indebted to their operation. Their relation to the material world is indeed so intimate that in one passage Philo speaks of the four elements as powers; "Earth, water, air, sun, moon, heavens, other incorporeal powers" form one continuous list. The powers are subject to no change. They are incomprehensible, known by their operation, not by their essential being. They are independent of time. They share many characteristics with the angels but are really a distinct and higher type of being. Primarily they are known to us through their operation as cosmic forces, but their energy is directed always by purpose and by providence and is not a blind activity. Rational and moral features also characterize them. It is through them that the will and the mind of God find expression. The powers are free from error, making no mistakes, adequate and perfectly adapted to their mediatory task.

At the head of all this wonderful hierarchy stands the Logos, and the Logos was the greatest of the conceptions which distinctively belong to the Alexandrine age. It will be best however to speak of the Logos in connection with Clement, whose teaching on the subject has affinity with Philo's, though it differs by being Christian. Leaving then this greatest of all the mediatory powers apart, we may examine the other members of the supra-mundane company. Their order and succession is less defined than was the case with the æons of Gnosticism, but to some extent they form a descending hierarchy. Philo identified his powers with the ideas of Plato, and like Plato did not confine these higher existences into rigid scheme and plan. They were indeed too numerous for arrangement. But in one passage he treats the six Cities of Refuge as allegorically representing the six highest powers. Three cities were beyond Jordan and represent the powers who control the heavens and the whole cosmic order. Three cities were on this side of Jordan, and these typify the agencies which are concerned with the life of man. This classification is incidental rather than maintained. Indeed the same passage arranges the six in a somewhat different scheme, placing the Logos at the head, apart, then assigning to the creative, regal and propitious powers their places next in order, finally completing the scheme by the inclusion of the preceptive and prohibitive powers, which are subdivisions of the legislative.

Elsewhere Philo tells us that once, as he meditated upon the subject of the Cherubim, it came to him by a flash of inspiration that these represent the two supreme and primary powers of God, his goodness and his authority. But the flaming sword was the symbol of the divine Logos, rapid and penetrating in its action. In another characteristic passage he deals with the Ten Commandments, and notes that God has left them as simple injunctions, with no penalties attached. The reason for this lies in the fact that Justice is ever God's assessor, seated by him, surveying human affairs and never failing to impose the penalty that is due. The Most High preserves his beneficence unalloyed. The minister sees that the offender does not escape. Again, Abraham entertained three angels. Here Philo finds a pre-Christian Trinity. For the centre figure represents the Father; on either side are the two powers, one creative, the other royal. So we have a trinity and a unity but the unity is the ultimate truth. As often, the essential elements of the divine being are spoken of as separate and independent and yet the unity is reasserted. On the other hand when the glory of the Lord is said to have rested on Mount Sinai the distinction is emphasized. It is not God in his essential nature who moves from place to place and "comes down", for we may not localize the real being of God. It is not the Lord but "*the glory of the Lord*" that is in question. The glory is subordinate, related, accessible to Moses in the mount, a mediate phase of the divine, able to be locally manifested without involving the self-existent in conditions of time and space. It is a characteristic idea of Philo's exegesis, for which many parallels may be found.

All who deal with Philo's theology discuss the question whether or no we have in all these powers and their various offices real mediation, whether Philo does consistently leave God in his transcendence and bridge the gap which separates God from the world by these intermediate agencies. As against this interpretation it is urged that these powers are in reality only the divine attributes, such as might, and love, and purpose, described as separately in action, without any intention on Philo's part to give them independent existence. The powers, it is said, are phases and modes of action rather than self-existent beings. Personification of the divine attributes was easy and natural in a poetical manner, without involving any definite theory of their independent existence. Moreover the very conception of personality was then so undetermined, that we are liable to read into language implications quite unintended by the writer. Allegory, too, lent facility to the process. If Sarah symbolized wisdom, it became more natural to think of Wisdom as a person. On such lines it has been contended that the independence of Philo's powers is really very slight, that essentially they are God's attributes, not ministers who act in the place of God.

Now it is in any case impossible to bring all Philo's teaching on this point into one consistent scheme. He is rhetorical and a ready writer and will at one time personify what elsewhere he treats as an attribute. What makes, however, his attitude in regard to mediating agencies clear is his deliberate assignment to the powers of tasks which he definitely refuses to leave in the hands of God. Two examples may suffice. God himself, Philo says, made the higher rational element in man. The lower items, whereby man is liable to error and to wickedness, were not God's work but are due to the subordinate agency of the powers. And Philo adds to justify this interpretation of the words "Let *us* make man" that it did not befit the dignity of God, the ruler of the universe, to make the road to wickedness in a rational soul by his own agency.

Consider, secondly, the matter of punishment. Even in the Old Testament it was said: "Whom the Lord loveth, he chasteneth." Punishment in Plato is always remedial, never vindictive. From the New Testament standpoint suffering is a discipline of love. But Philo shrinks from allowing that punishment is the act of God. God, he says, is the cause of all that is best; he does what is akin to his own nature. "But punishments appointed for the wicked are inflicted by means of his subordinate ministers." Three visitors came to Abraham in his tent at Mamre, one of whom represented the supreme God. Only two came to Sodom to announce its impending destruction, for his powers, but not God himself, discharge the task of discipline and bring about deserved calamity. Generals and ministers organize war and impose penalties. But the Great King sets his hands to no such task. He is apart; peace and security and riches and all good things are of his giving, for such is his nature. If severity and conflict and retribution are in question, that is the work of his subordinate ministers. We have something like an anticipation of Marcion's separation of the good God from the stern Creator and Lawgiver.

It is clear from these passages that the powers act in accordance with the divine will, yet that their action is their own. They are subordinate but relatively independent, and when they punish, or introduce error, they do what may not be described as due to the act of God. The deity abides in uncontaminated goodness. His moral isolation is as complete for Philo as his ontological isolation is for Plotinus. If other agencies accomplish needful tasks which are inappropriate to the innate purity of the divine nature, clearly we must abandon all right to describe such beings as merely attributes of God. Their power of initiative is too definitely asserted. The holiness of the powers remains unstained, for they are ministers of the Most High, but essentially they are subordinate, mediating agencies, bringing the will of the Unrelated into contact with the world and lower things. Philo's conception is a noble one, fusing Hellenic with Hebrew elements, and giving us a vision of a vast company which no man can number or fully understand, who in time and throughout the universe, and also beyond these limits, are God's ministers and rejoice in their service, holding the stars upon their courses, giving the flowers their beauty and their movement to the waters, and endowing with their highest faculties the mind and soul of man. But the character of mediation lies upon all their work. They hold the universe in unity. They bring what is beyond into relation with what is here. They secure the immunity of God and yet make manifest his nature. Not "one mediator between God and man" but a host of intermediate existences.

Clement's doctrine of the Logos is perhaps the highest and richest expression of this theory of mediation. It dominates his theology and has religious as well as theological value. "The Word, who is common to both, is Mediator, Son of God, Saviour of men, God's minister, our Teacher." Clement takes over all Philo's teaching on the cosmic offices of the Word, not diminishing the area of the Word's administration by the introduction of subordinate powers. The clause in the Nicene Creed which says of the second Person of the Trinity: "By whom all things were made", is with Clement a constant theme; δι' οὗ, by whom, through whom, is a phrase of constant recurrence. Like the Wisdom of the Old Testament the Word is the Counsellor of God in the fashioning of the universe; he is also instrument, minister, agent. The Johannine text, "Without him was not anything made", is abundantly employed and expanded. All the principalities and powers of the spiritual world, all the stars of heaven upon their courses, the history of the world and the life of man, are alike originated and regulated by the Word. Thus he writes in a characteristic passage: "Most perfect, most holy, most sovereign, most supreme, most royal, most beneficent is the nature of the Son, which stands nearest to the One Almighty. He is the greatest exaltation; he orders all things according to the will of the Father and steers the universe excellently, effecting by his unworn, unwearying power, all things whereby he accomplishes the hidden purposes of the Father as he discerns them. For never does the Son of God move from his watch tower. He is not divided. He is not cut off. He moves not from place to place. Everywhere and always in being and never circumscribed, he is entirely mind, entirely the light paternal, entirely vision, seeing all and searching the powers by his power. Unto him, as unto the Word of the Father who has received this holy administration by reason of him who has subjected them, is made subject the host of angels and of gods, through whom also all men belong unto him, though some belong by full knowledge, others not yet in the same degree, others as friends, others as faithful servants, others as servants simply."

Less distinctively Clement's but still one of his favourite themes is the office of the Word as Revealer of God. Revelation is by the Son. He is the Herald of the King. The countenance of the Father is made manifest in the Son. Only through the Logos may we know God. In this connection the Incarnation and the Lord's human life have special significance. The Alexandrines always undervalued history, but even Clement writes of the earthly advent as a wonderful event, and speaks in terms of which Tertullian would not have disapproved of the astonishing spread of the Christian religion through the world. Institutions in this connection have their value, so church and ministry and sacraments are important for Clement, all effective in so far as they are under the Word's control.

And this leads us to yet another office of the Mediator-Word. De Faye says of Clement that he was "Foncièrement pédagogue", at heart the teacher. He was certainly more at home in the lecture room than in a church, and his interest in his pupils finds varied expression in his pages. All this sense of his own high calling he transfers to his conception of the Word as the great Educator of humanity. This is essentially a religious element in his thought. He sees life as a divinely ordered system of training for the human soul. There are stages, there are the several subjects in their order, there are the various lines of approach, but in all the Word is operative, leading men upwards, pointing the road towards final vision, deeming nothing unimportant and no man wholly incapable of higher things. Greek philosophy and the Old Testament were converging roads of progress which met in the highway of Christianity. Each had its place in the scheme of the divine Educator, so that Plato as well as Moses led their followers towards the Kingdom of God. Such teaching was indeed catholic in the highest sense, and was in that age probably only possible in Alexandria.

Within the Christian scheme such training has its stages. Like the Lord himself Clement loved children, and delighted to regard mankind as God's children under the training of the Word. It is the Word's office to inspire, to warn, to encourage, to guide, to point the way. In each of these tasks the Word is ever tender and considerate, and where there is discipline it is always the discipline of love. The Word is all things to the children in his care: πάντα τῷ νηπίῳ ὁ λόγος, entering into the details of life, so that in Clement's *Pædagogus* we have directions as to the right kind of shoes, the use of flowers, the occasions which justify the wearing of a ring and the ways in which married people should live together. In Clement's day converts were coming into the Church in great numbers. Many of them, as we know, had hardly counted the cost before baptism, and soon found it difficult to shed by one sharp decision the pleasanter ways of paganism. So we may imagine, after listening to one of Clement's lectures, a newly-converted Christian girl asking herself: "Does the Word really expect me never to wear my pretty robe with flowers painted on it?" or some young man much puzzled by being told that he must never go to the theatre and only rarely take a bath.

These were early stages. The divine Teacher had greater things in store for the Christian, and Clement gives us, in his account of the Christian Gnostic, one of the highest types of saintly character. The Christian who has so far attained passes from faith to knowledge. He has learned apathy, to be indifferent to lower things. Now that his earlier stages of purification are over, he is initiated into the mysteries of the higher life and moves onwards towards his goal. Yet he does not wholly lose his human interests, for he does good, will even accept a public office, is ever courteous and is ever ready to impart to others lessons he has learned himself. But he moves on an ascending way, seeking at last to be conducted by the divine Educator, who has now become for him the Great High Priest, into the shrine where perfect vision, the uninterrupted communion of the soul, are his final reward. The stages of education have ended in abiding peace.

In Clement's Logos, whose offices as Creator, Revealer, Educator, have been described, we have mediation in its highest, fullest stage. The Logos dominates and pervades Clement's teaching. The Supreme Deity remains apart in his remote transcendence. The Spirit is still doctrinally unimportant, and indeed every task that was ever assigned to the Spirit is already fully discharged by the Logos. Clement's *Hymn to the Word* leaves no occasion for any "Veni Creator". So we are left with the conception of an august mediatorial Person, who was Counsellor and Agent of the Most High in the making of the world, who is the Vice-gerent and Administrator of God throughout the ages, who is the unchanging dynamic force in all the changes of time, who has ever been the Educator and Guardian of humanity, who is the Reason and Mind of God, manifest in the universe and once also in a perfect human life. Much is to be learned from this thought of a supreme Mediator, even though the thought belonged to Clement's age, and did not maintain its dominant position in the later development of Christian theology.

Origen's greatest contribution to the theory of mediation is his doctrine of the Eternal Generation of the Son. The being and nature of the Son or Word are derived from the supreme Father, but the derivation is not in time; it is an abiding, an essential relationship. For God cannot be Father if there be no Son; God cannot be omnipotent if there be no Word through whose instrumentality he effects his will. So we come to the famous saying, really Origen's, that there never was a time when the Son did not exist. If it is true that the idea of a Son presupposes that of a Father, such pre-existence is logical only, in no sense temporal. Origen's favourite illustration for this relationship is that of light and its radiance. The two cannot be dissociated. Light is not light if it sheds no radiance; radiance there is none apart from the light which is its source. Yet within the unity there is derivation. The rays can be distinguished from their source. The Father is ingenerate, the Son is generated being. But again this relationship is timeless, abiding, eternal. The principle of mediation is not lost. Absolute being is not the property of the Son. We are in the first phase of the process by which we pass from the One to the many, though in distinguishing light from its radiance we have reduced the distinction to its lowest possible term.

Origen makes his position clear by associating his doctrine with one well-known item in the thought of his time and contrasting it with another. The Old Testament conception of Wisdom had been prominent in Philo. Origen had a liking for the books which we include in our Apocrypha, so he goes not to the Proverbs or the book of Job but to the Alexandrine Book of Wisdom, where it is said of Wisdom that she is "a breath of the power of God and a clear effluence of the glory of the Almighty; she is an effulgence from everlasting light, and an unspotted mirror of the working of God and an image of his goodness". The language, Origen argues, implies that Wisdom is not something accessory or additional to the divine nature but an element in the very being of God, and he identifies Wisdom with the Son. He is familiar with the statement in the book of Proverbs that the Lord created Wisdom in the beginning of his ways, but he ignores the implication, which was to shock the orthodox later on, that the Son so would be a creature. For Origen Wisdom is identical with the Word and his doctrine of eternal generation owes much to the earlier teaching of the Old Testament books.

But with the rival Gnostic theory Origen will make no peace. Though he will describe the Son as the radiance, power, or goodness of God, still he is a separate hypostasis, has a being and existence of his own, derivative yet independent. The

Gnostic theory of emanation, the view that the Word was merely the uttered expression of the mind of God, all teaching which reduced the Son to the position of an attribute or characteristic and denied his personality, Origen, with all his willingness to consider alternative theories, decisively rejects. The doctrine of the Trinity, still far from final definition, clearly reaches a further stage of development in Origen. Implicitly, had the Church realized all that it involved, his doctrine of eternal generation not only brought to an end the Adoptionist Christology, of which the Acts of the Apostles retain many traces, but also by anticipation provided the answer to the later teaching of Arius. Still, it is our present interest to note that essentially Origen's doctrine is a particular phase of the principle of mediation. Even "God of God" implies it.

Two other elements in Origen's teaching are of interest in this connection. They may be indicated even though we have not time for full discussion.

In contrast with the unbroken unity of the divine nature in its highest essence, Origen has much to say of the manifold offices of the Word. The thought has its religious value; the Son has many tasks since human nature has many needs. He is saviour, since man needs salvation; he is physician, since souls are sick; he is our ransom, since we are in captivity. The Son has many names, and Origen is surprised that so many Christians thought of him simply as the "Word" and ignored the rich significance of his many other titles. The Gospels, Epistles, and even the earlier Prophets give abundant evidence of this manifold character of the Son. There is no requirement of our higher nature which the Son for our sakes is not prepared to meet. But there is an order of development and they are happy who need him no longer as a shepherd, physician or ransom, but who are able to welcome him as wisdom, word, or righteousness, or in whatever other capacity he is known to the souls who have so far advanced. This idea of the manifold Christ is suggestive and valuable.

But if the Word was man's friend, there were also in the same intermediate status terrible enemies. The demons were only too real to Origen. A whole chapter in the *De Principiis* is devoted to the subject of these unseen adversaries, whose existence both Old and New Testaments abundantly illustrate. Originally fallen spirits, beings who lost their high estate through infirmity of will, they are still active agencies of evil, incorporeal, yet earthbound, haunting every foul abode, instigating man to sin and wickedness, specially intent on driving him to blaspheme his maker and charge God with unrighteousness. Origen speaks of the whole subject as a wide and difficult study, and as one in which rash assertion by the uninformed was specially dangerous. It is a constant topic of controversy in his argument with Celsus, but the notable fact in all his references is that he never questions the reality of these lesser powers of evil. Their existence is never a matter for debate. Their terrible influence is amply admitted. They would be too strong for human nature but for the protecting power of God's grace. For some reason they are permitted by God, and their malign influence will not have ultimate success. Even already the departed souls of the martyrs join issue with these unseen adversaries and the demons lose the day.

Demonology is a very wide subject and for Origen a very real one. There were spiritual powers of wickedness in high places, many in number, varied in their grades, consistently the foes of man. For with Origen, as in the New Testament, these powers are always evil. All the demons were bad, he thought. In that they differed from the angels. Origen's beliefs should be compared with the two Orations of Maximus of Tyre on the Demon or Genius of Socrates. There these powers are regarded as beneficent or friendly. They are "secondary immortals", many of them disembodied souls, a great company, and heroes like Hector and Achilles have their place among the rest. Indeed the demons here approximate in their office to the saints and angels of the Church. But with Origen they are always adverse, evil powers, with whom man must wrestle, as actual as in later days the devil was actual to Luther or St. Dunstan. These are mediate beings of the darker sort.

In the scheme of Clement and Origen the Logos is the link between God and the world. The whole mediatorial office tends to be concentrated in the hands of this one Person, who is adequate to its highest and its lowest tasks. There is one mediator, or at least one is predominantly active. In the scheme of Plotinus there are two grades of mediation; one belongs to "$Νοῦς$", Mind or Spirit, the other to Soul. The system is more definitely trinitarian than that of the Christian Fathers; it is also more definitely a system of subordination. From the One to the Spirit is a descent; there is a further descent from the Spirit to the Soul. To these three Plotinus will have no addition. There is no room for two Spirits. The Soul, though differentiated into many particular souls, is still ever one in principle. His upper world is not crowded with any manifold hierarchy of being and he definitely charges Gnosticism with introducing an unending and unnecessary series of divine minds. The Supreme is a triad, no more.

The One is the source of Spirit, if we are to accept Inge's choice of the term 'spirit' as the nearest equivalent we have for νοῦς. Spirit is intuitive reason, an activity which is eternal, for we have not descended yet to time, and which knows and contemplates without process or discursive reasoning. It is an intermediate and all-embracing consciousness of reality. In its action are no stages, no before or after. It is therefore free from all change or confusion. Plotinus has to reconcile the idea of rest with that of action. His spirit creates and yet is free from change. It has no needs and yet it is a constant activity. The seeming opposition of these ideas is overcome when we realize that the activity of Spirit is essentially internal. Its life is not only timeless, it is also self-contained. Its contemplation is within the circle of its own being. It is a wheel revolving around its own centre, at once stationary and in movement. And yet it is no colourless unvaried existence for Spirit holds all forms and ideas, in the Platonic sense, as its own. "The doctrine of Plotinus is that so far as every thought in Spirit is also an eternal form, all the thoughts of Spirit are ideas. Spirit embraces all the ideas, as the whole its parts. Each idea is Spirit and Spirit is the totality of the ideas."

It was a well-known saying of Aristotle that the soul is realities or being: ἡ ψυχή ἐστί πως τὰ ὄντα.

This is what Plotinus teaches in regard to Spirit. It is Spirit that gives subsistence to the things that are. It is τὰ ὄντα. It perceives realities in itself as being itself. Spirit and Being are really one. The three terms Spirit (νοῦς) its activity, (νόησις) its object (νοητόν), really describe a whole, for the unity between Spirit and its object is closer than that implied when we say that subject and object necessitate one another, or when νοῦς and τὸ νοητόν are spoken of as correlative, or when we say that the mind makes nature. It is difficult to grasp the full significance of the plain terms Plotinus uses. We are of course in a world which is timeless and incorporeal, and here he tells us that Spirit and its object of thought are really one. Spirit thus is being. The spiritual world is not, in spacial language, outside spirit. What mind knows mind is, and what is is due to mind. We have here the first stage of transition from the One, which is above being. Νοῦς, Mind, Spirit, is being. Here is the earliest phase of mediation.

If we find it difficult to grasp in all its intimate unity this fusion of Spirit and its objects, we may remember that wise men have admitted that beyond the threshold of the eternal world principles prevail which logic is powerless to analyse. In any case the highest activity of Spirit is a stage nearer to us than the unbroken unity of the One. And at times Plotinus seems to welcome the greater wealth of being which this descent from the Absolute makes possible. He says for example of the Spirit: "It is beautiful; the most beautiful of all; lying lapped in pure light and in clear radiance; circumscribing the nature of the real existences; the original of which this beautiful world is a shadow and an image; tranquil in the fulness of glory, since in it there is nothing devoid of Spirit, nothing dark or out of rule; a living thing in a life of blessedness. This too must overwhelm with awe any that has seen it, and penetrated it, to become a unit of its being."

From Spirit we pass to Soul. It is again a descent. Spirit is prior to Soul, beyond the world, while Soul may be within it. The world-soul, the *anima mundi*, is the lowest stage of the ideal and spiritual world. Caird speaks of soul as distinguished from spirit or the intelligence in so far as in it the difference of one idea from another is more definitely actualized. In other words the soul is further from the One and nearer to the many. It is indeed itself a manifold, for the world-soul breaks up into particular souls. The soul never wholly leaves the higher sphere. It remains unchangeable there, participating in the Supreme, yet streams forth ceaselessly, life issuing from life, an energy running through the universe, so that there is no extremity at which it wholly fades. Itself incorporeal it can come into association with matter, and from soul matter receives its form. Thus soul and matter co-operate to produce determinate being, for matter itself is formless and indeterminate, and the office of soul is to impart form. Association with matter may corrupt the soul, so that it becomes unclean and ugly and acquires passions by too intimate converse with the body, but in its proper function soul redeems matter from its evil and imparts to it whatever is possible of the good. Thus soul is the active power in the creation of the universe and in its maintenance. It is with the universe that Time comes into being, so that time is only possible through the soul. In itself the soul is immortal, both the world soul and the soul of the individual, which is capable of existing apart from the body and may be reincarnate in another existence. In the scheme of Plotinus the soul plays a large and varied part. Its range is from intimate association with pure spirit to equally intimate association with matter. It is a medium, a middle term, the link between the intelligible and the sensible worlds. How largely Alexandrine views of the universe were dominated by the principles of mediation is abundantly evident in the teaching of Plotinus on the soul. In the Christian Trinity the emphasis lies on the second

Person; in the Neoplatonic it falls on the third.

In all these theories of mediâtion the aim is to connect the One and the many, to relate God and the world, to show how Spirit comes into contact with material existence, to overcome contrast and opposition by a graduated scale of being. The intermediate beings, whether described as Aeons or Powers, as Spirit or as Logos, whether numerous as in one school, or restricted as in another, are always characterized by one determining feature. The order of their succession is a descending order. There are successive grades of being, but the whole process is a degradation. We pass from unity to multiplicity, from the good to the less good. More and more, as we approach the material, form is limited by matter. The lower spiritual agencies can do what it would be impiety to attribute to the higher. To be born into an individual human existence involves a descent for the soul. And in the macrocosm as in the microcosm the sensible world is lower than the spiritual world, and creation comes by the decline of the soul into association with matter. Thus it is no evolution which the Alexandrines offer us. At times they are willing to praise the wonder and beauty of the world and to regard the Creator as rejoicing in the glory of his handiwork. Such statements are not easy to reconcile with the theory so consistently held that the whole process is one of descent, from which indeed there is to be ultimate recovery, but which still involves transition from the higher to the lower and the lower. The recoil from material things, a recoil which seems to be excessive, involves a lowered estimate of the world of sense. The cosmic process is not one of expanding grandeur, of ordered and wonderful amplification. Instead we are told that in each successive astral circle something is lost, that the soul contracts impurities on its downward journey, that the higher constantly generates but that it generates a lower, lesser thing, that inherently the manifold must be inferior to the one. Origen, who in some ways is less troubled by the thought of evil than many other teachers, still regards creation as a descent. He makes much of the Greek term, καταβολή, "foundation", and insists upon its implication of descent and inferiority. God, as it were, laid down the foundations of the cosmos, and the divine action so worked downwards into a lower sphere. And, to name Origen again, those of his interpreters who hold that he teaches the subordination of the Logos are probably right, however much Origen also said to exalt the Word to consubstantiality and co-eternity. Still, "The Father is greater than I". With many points of difference these Alexandrine teachers are fundamentally at one in this that they all regard the cosmic process as one of subordination and deterioration. This process starts in the spiritual world and is continued in the sensible and material. The extremes are on the one hand God, the One; on the other, formless matter. Theories of mediation supply the connection but the process is essentially a descent. We may say that an element of pessimism is involved. At any rate the problem of evil is not ignored.

This descent in the scale of being may be considered in connection with the doctrine of the Fall. The recent Bampton Lectures of Professor N. P. Williams have brought this subject again to notice, and have in particular shown the entire inadequacy of the solution provided by the biblical story of Adam's sin. Even if Adam be regarded as typical of humanity as a whole, the explanation offered in the story does not suffice, for to trace all evil to the frailty of the human will is unfair to man and does not really relieve the Creator of all responsibility. The lectures in question have much to say in regard to Origen's teaching on the subject. We are invited to leave Augustine and to return to Origen. There are also some comments of great interest on the position of Plotinus.

We must not follow these suggestions in detail. One point only is here to be noted. The Professor's position is this, that the cause of evil in man would seem to be historically prior to man, and that its genesis may be accounted for by the hypothesis of a pre-mundane vitiation of the whole life force, at the very beginning of cosmic evolution. This suggestion that evil is due to a pre-mundane fall may claim support from those Alexandrine teachers whose theories of mediation we have considered. Whether a conscious life force, an *anima mundi*, the world-soul of Plotinus, fell like the Gnostic Sophia by a wrong exercise of freedom, or whether, as a less personal supposition, we must regard all procession as inherently involving inferiority so that what comes forth from the Ultimate must have within it an element of imperfection—in either case we cannot start our explanation with:

"Man's first disobedience, and the fruit
Of that forbidden tree, whose mortal taste
Brought death into the world, and all our woe."

At a stage immeasurably earlier, in a sphere purely spiritual, while time still was not, where history fails us altogether and only imagination can be our guide, in some manner transcendental and incomprehensible, the decline began. How? It is vain to ask. Neither the ancient Alexandrines nor the modern Professor can tell us or explain. But we may agree with both that it was not all Adam's doing, nor even Eve's.

This short course has already run to half its length. For two lectures we have been occupied in the world of mind or spirit, as the Alexandrines conceived it, and have not yet arrived at the visible universe of things which can be seen and measured. Our justification must be that the Alexandrines lived themselves largely in the κόσμος νοητός, in the heavenly or intelligible sphere. Origen knew more about angels and demons than he did about human beings. Clement was more interested in the Logos than in the historic Son of Man. Plotinus regarded time as just an image of eternity. Philo was impatient when circumstances led him to interrupt his mystical interpretation of Scripture and travel on a political embassy to Rome. It is no exaggeration to say of these men that they spent half their time in the spiritual world.

Did their contemplations profit them? Was the outcome of their supra-mundane interest an outlook less or more optimistic than our own? Did they believe that the universe was friendly, and if so had they better grounds for their belief than are possible for us? Was their world-view, their "Welt-anschauung", more confident and serene than that of the man who has read and understood what Eddington and Jeans and Whitehead have told us in recent years?

Points of similarity in the old view and the new way may be discovered. It was agreed then and is agreed now that the ultimate reality lies beyond the reach of man. It was agreed then and it has not been denied now that spirit or reason operates in the constitution of the universe. Both the Alexandrines and our scientists somewhat minimize the importance of man in the cosmic scheme; neither school is anthropocentric. The whole ancient world, and especially that section of it which went back through Plato to Pythagoras, believed in the property of numbers. So modern physics seem to be fundamentally mathematical.

In like manner we might draw contrasts. The ancients had imagination; the moderns have experiment and calculation. The ultimate forces for the ancients tended to be personal. Into this category you cannot bring radiation or an electron. The ancients clung to the past; the moderns are heading towards the future. But in one respect the ancient interpretation was perhaps the happier. There was more correspondence for them between the character of the ultimate powers they believed in and the higher elements in human nature than is at present possible through the scientific interpretation of the world. From Plato to Plotinus the supreme power is good. The Creator had some beneficent purpose in willing that the world shall be. The Logos was loving as well as rational. The world soul had moral qualities. The ultimate reality was that which we all desire, to which in a measure we are akin. When the time process is at an end Origen could feel confident, "God shall be all in all".

The new science is not concerned to deny the modern equivalent of such a view. It leaves indeed far more possibility for these convictions than the old mechanical view of nature seemed to admit. But it gives us little sanction for them. Eddington writes: "The idea of a universal Mind or Logos would be, I think, a fairly plausible inference from the present state of scientific theory; at least it is in harmony with it. But if so, all that our enquiry justifies us in asserting is a purely colourless pantheism. Science cannot tell whether the world-spirit is good or evil, and its halting argument for the existence of a God might equally well be turned into an argument for the existence of a Devil." As for ourselves, humanity, Jeans writes: "Our earth is so infinitesimal in comparison with the whole universe; we, the only thinking beings, so far as we know, in the whole of space, are to all appearances so accidental, so far removed from the main scheme of the universe, that it is *a priori* all too probable that any meaning that the universe as a whole may have, would entirely transcend our terrestrial experience, and so be totally unintelligible to us."

There is nothing then in the spaces or the ages to promote an ultimate optimism or to forbid it. Truly we are strangers and pilgrims, if not intruders. The universe is fair rather than friendly. The ultimate powers seem colourless, cold, indifferent, unconcerned. We must fall back for faith and optimism upon the voices that speak within. Perhaps the ancients had more assurance from external sources than the new science can sanction for ourselves. The link between God and man is mathematical. It may be also spiritual and moral, but the new science, to which all the world is now looking, cannot say so. Plotinus did say so. Origen did. Christ did.

LECTURE III

THE UNIVERSE

We must descend now from the spiritual world to the material. From the unseen powers of the intelligible or spiritual order, whether original or mediate, the scheme of these lectures will lead us to ask what in the lower sphere of sight and sense the Alexandrines thought about the earth and the stars and the time process, the constitution of things material and the things that are to come. From which in the next and concluding lecture we shall go on to consider their views on man.

In regard to the physical universe it cannot be claimed that these teachers had any very notable contribution to make. They are far more original in their treatment of the unseen world than in their views of the world we see. Imagination, rather than observation, guided their interest, and in their estimate of material things they are more dependent than in their spiritual teaching on the schemes and theories of their predecessors. The older masters had great influence. Not so much the opinion as the man who held it carried weight. The cosmogony of the Alexandrines and their interpretations of the cosmic process depended in particular upon what had been taught already in the first chapters of Genesis, in the *Timaeus* of Plato and by various leaders of the Stoic school. We may regret that in their use of the early chapters of Genesis the Alexandrine Platonists, both Jewish and Christian, were diverted by their love of allegory from closer attention to the physical aspects of that wonderful narrative. All of them had much to say about it. Origen wrote commentaries and delivered homilies on Genesis, and the "Six Days" became a standing topic for patristic comment. Philo too brings the narrative into relation with current philosophic ideas, and the same combination is found even earlier in the book of Wisdom. The writer of the narrative of the creation is realistic and objective in his outlook, severely refusing place to speculation or interpretation. His version of the story of the earliest things, however much in origin it owed to prior Babylonian accounts, is given with authority and allows few open questions. But in many of its items the narrative of Genesis admitted of an exegesis which harmonized with distinctively Alexandrine teaching.

The visible world has a spiritual origin. God is a creator, not only a maker who fashions pre-existing material into such shapes as he desires. Moreover, creation is by an act of will. It is not from prior fate or necessity or chance, nor yet by a process of emanation or involuntary self-expression. Also, in spite of the prevailing monotheism, plurality is found in the divine nature. Much, as we have had previous occasion to note, is made by the interpreters of the text: "Let us make man".

Matter, in the writer's view, was not eternally pre-existent. It was created, but in a chaotic state, "Tohu wa—bohu", without form and void, so that there were later stages in the process of creation by which the undetermined, uncharacterized element was brought into form and order and became fit material for the more developed results. Some affinity may be seen here between the teaching of Genesis and other teaching on the constitution of matter which will come under our notice later on. The heavenly bodies are for seasons; days and months and years depend on their movements, so that time itself may be said to begin with the creation of the world. They are also "for signs", and the use of the term "sign" is important in view of the widespread belief in astrology and in the possibility of reading the secrets of the future in the book of the heavens. But when we read, "He made the stars *also*", as though they were an unimportant addition to the greater and lesser lights, we have the survival of an earlier view, for great importance is consistently attached by the

Alexandrines to the stars. For Origen as for Plotinus they were among the important factors of the cosmos. In the main the narrative of the garden supports the view that evil is due to a defect of will. Desire directed to wrong ends caused the fall. And yet this is not the whole explanation, for the serpent was already there, so that the trouble was older than human nature. But the original creation was good. The question whether a perfect God can create an imperfect world had not arisen as yet. "God saw everything that he had made and behold it was very good." Only with a certain reserve did the Alexandrines adopt this opinion.

The account of the making of the world in Plato's *Timaeus* is the Hellenic parallel to Genesis. The dialogue has had greater vogue and influence than any other work of Plato except possibly the *Republic*. There is a Pythagorean element in it, and in considerable sections it is definitely mathematical. Many of the problems which Alexandrine writers discuss make their earlier appearance in this dialogue.

The *Timaeus* does not claim assured certainty for its teaching. The account it gives of the making of the world is said to be probable, none possessing more likelihood than this. Human limitations forbid any higher claim to full knowledge and exact. But, with this proviso, the *Timaeus* gives us a fairly complete cosmogony. The universe has come into existence. It is visible and tangible and all things of this nature are generated and not eternal. The Creator, the Demiurgos, who brought it into being, is by nature good, and he created this visible universe after a heavenly pattern; it is the image or copy of a higher cosmos that is unseen. As for the motive which led God to make the world, it was his goodness. Knowing no envy God desired all should be good, so he brought this wonderful universe into being. "He brought it into order out of disorder, deeming that the former state is in all ways better than the latter." Perhaps Plato meant that before God made the world, a chaotic, unformed, unordered material already existed, teaching so the eternity of matter. He has much to say of this unqualified, characterless and purely receptive substance of which the four elements and the whole cosmic structure are formed, but the question of its eternity is not clear. In any case the Creator fashioned reason within the soul and placed soul within the body of the universe, so that the Cosmos was a living creature endowed with soul and reason owing to the providence of God.

Plato's universe is one. It is a single living creature. In shape it is spherical, for a sphere is the most perfect form. Time came into being together with the universe, and time imitates eternity. In its generation an element of necessity blends with reason, but necessity does not violate the harmony of the order. It is to be noted that in Plato the supreme God creates. He is maker and father of the universe. He is responsible for the whole, and the whole is good. But for the structure of mortal things, lesser divinities take action. The sons of God, the powers who are subordinate, make the bodies of mortal creatures. This is the task of the younger gods, so that God himself may abide in his proper state, and the responsibility for inferior creatures, including man, remains with the secondary divinities. Deterioration is possible; there is disease and there is folly, but the account as a whole is optimistic as its concluding words may show:

"And now at length we may say that our discourse concerning the Universe has reached its termination. For this our Cosmos has received the living creatures both mortal and immortal and been thereby fulfilled; it being itself a visible Living Creature embracing the visible creatures, a perceptible God made in the image of the Intelligible, most great and good and fair and perfect in its generation—even this one heaven sole of its kind."

The Stoic school had its representatives in

Alexandria in the period with which we are concerned. Chaeremon, Nero's tutor, taught there and had a considerable following. After him a certain Dionysius, a man of letters rather than a philosopher, also taught Stoic doctrine in Alexandria. But the real home of Stoicism in the first and second centuries was not in the east but in Rome, where Seneca and Marcus Aurelius brought its ethical and religious elements into prominence. Its cosmological theory, which at the moment is our concern, was however widely known and must have been familiar to every teacher of any standing in Alexandria.

Stoic influence and Stoic terminology are to be found in all the leading writers of the period, and where the tenets of Zeno and Chrysippus were not accepted, they were frequently the cause of fuller development and expression in the opposite or alternative doctrine, much as the doctrine of the Christian Church was largely formulated through the contest with the heresies of Gnosticism. Of the more prominent elements in the Stoic scheme one was definitely rejected by the Alexandrines, another was adopted and assimilated by at least one distinguished master of the Platonic school.

The Stoics were materialists. They avoided the dualism of mind and matter, of being and becoming, by making God coterminous with material substance, and by identifying reality with what had extension, bulk, position, solidity. The term οὐσία, being, meant for the Stoic something corporeal. The soul was conceived as a body. There was no ideal humanity apart from the particular, individual, concrete man. The intelligible, spiritual, world, the κόσμος νοητός, has no place in the Stoic universe. It is on the principles of the lower realism we must base our interpretation of the world.

But this materialism was qualified. Matter admitted of grades of solidity. From the most concrete and solid substances there was a rising scale of refinement and tenuity, till in its most rarefied stages matter became almost indistinguishable from mind and spirit. Earth, water, air, fire, are an ascending scale of rarefaction. The fifth element, in which Aristotle believed, might have formed another link in the chain which connects mind and matter, but the Stoics were content with fire and endowed it with such qualities as reason, wisdom, purpose, and the like. God for them was body in its last degree of tenuity. The fiery æther, of such elemental rarity that it seemed wholly freed from the solidity of matter, was rational and was divine, and in this sense God was immanent in the world, permeating all things and in the last resort making matter God. This is the pantheism of the Stoics. How far their theory was from what we understand by materialism may be best seen in the first of Mr. Edwyn Bevan's four lectures on *Stoics and Sceptics*. "The whole of the Stoic physics," it is said, "was directed to showing that the power operative in the Universe was rational: all its theory of the constitution of the material world and the course of its movement led up to that crowning result."

Nevertheless the Platonists would not come to terms. It shocks Clement; it is a sheer disgrace to philosophy to think of God as permeating even the basest material elements. As we have seen, the divine must at all costs be protected from such contact, even though the result be utter isolation. Origen knows how rarefied and etherial was the spiritual fire of Stoicism, but it is, he urges, in the last resort a bodily substance, and he is at pains to show that when the Christians speak of God as breath or spirit or as fire, they use these terms without any corporeal implication; the language is only figurative. In general the Platonists in their reaction from the Stoic doctrine of immanence and materialism were led in the direction of the dualistic alternative. Their lack of interest in the concrete, their depreciation of matter, their indifference to events, their belief that the visible world should be shunned and avoided rather than enjoyed, their lack of what we should term scientific interest, for which after all Alexandria did offer large opportunities, all arose in some degree from their fear of contamination through contact with the world of sense, in which the very Stoic teaching they suspected was actively discovering significance and value.

In that respect the Stoic influence was by way of occasioning reaction. In other ways the Platonists were willing to learn. The Stoic Sage reappears both in Clement and in Plotinus. More notable still is the affinity between the cosmic cycles of Stoicism and Origen's doctrine of many worlds. Periodically, when the revolution was complete, the Stoic theory taught that the whole universe was dissolved in fire and a new order reconstituted similar to the old. It was not a matter of advancing process or of cosmic evolution. The cycle went round and round again. Hercules would again perform his labours, and Anytus and Meletus would again accuse Socrates of corrupting the youth, and so once again the wheel would come full circle. To us it all seems very aimless. Origen at least adds an element of hope and progress in his long vista and series of many worlds. But the whole conception of such a cosmic succession as we find it in Christian speculation was largely derived from the earlier teaching of Zeno, Cleanthes and Chrysippus.

Such were the main elements of speculative theory in regard to the physical world upon which the Alexandrine Platonists had to work. It is not to be claimed for them that they produced any new and original cosmology. Their task was accomplished within the area of accepted tradition, but even allowing these limits they found open questions and interest still attaches to their diversities of view.

How comes it that a world exists? Before we ask *what* the universe is, *why* is it? Of its nature we may know a little, but what are we to say about its origin? And the only real reply to that question is the Lord's answer to Job out of the whirlwind: "Where wast thou when I laid the foundations of the earth? Declare if thou hast understanding." And indeed Alexandrine teachers were not slow to declare their views. One supposition they were unanimous in excluding. The physical world did not exist for itself, on its own account. Whatever the link between matter and spirit, between being and becoming, the world of sense was not independent, self-sufficient, self-explanatory. From atoms alone you could not build a cosmic order. The things seen are in some way related to the things unseen; this principle holds as much for

Plotinus as for St. Paul. The Epicureans were indeed a discredited school and not to be taken seriously. They were largely ignored.

According to the Gnostics the material world was a deplorable mistake. One of the Æons, Sophia, fell by her unholy curiosity, and out of the pangs and pains of her frustrated desire arose matter, which was fashioned by the demiurgos into this lower world. The demiurge is a frequent figure in Gnostic speculation. He is partly minister, partly rival, of the supreme God, and the shadow of inferiority always rests upon his work. So the visible world ought never to have arisen. Extreme people even held the devil must have made it. All the beauty and the wonder of nature made no appeal to the Marcionites or the Valentinians. The universe was a faulty copy made by an incompetent artist of the world that is higher and invisible. Plotinus is on sure ground when he scolds the Gnostics for their indifference to the wonders of creation. He has no patience with these people who cavil at the universe. The world is the best possible. The things of sense can never reach the level of spiritual essences but, admitting this limitation, could any fabric be more excellent than the universe we know?

The physical world is not self-existent, nor is it the result of error. Its origin is good. The many come from the one. What is *here* was also *there*. The spiritual world is the original, but the visible world is at least as good and fair a copy as the material admits. What is the exact process by which the universe first arose? In what relation does spirit stand to rock and stone and trees?

One theory is creation, the action of the divine will which brings into being out of nothing that which previously did not exist. We can form no clear conception of creation in this absolute and unqualified sense, for we have no experience of creation out of nothing. But the thing can be stated, if it cannot be understood, and is so stated in the opening words of Genesis. God there does not work upon pre-existing material. The material, with the form it takes, are alike brought into being. Of the teachers we are considering Origen alone holds the doctrine of creation in this absolute sense. In many respects he departs from the Mosaic cosmogony but in the fundamental principle of creation *ex nihilo* he is biblical and uncompromising.

Two alternatives to this rigid account of the world's origin were possible and often found favour with the Alexandrines. The universe, instead of being brought into being by the fiat of an almighty Creator, might issue from the nature of divine being, as a stream from its source, the process being regarded as gradual and in the nature of things. Instead of a sudden and instantaneous "Let there be light and there was light", we should say "Light is of God because God himself is light". Something of this kind is in the Gnostic theory of emanation. The procession of the Holy Ghost is perhaps a parallel from Christian theology. Successive phases of being in an orderly process, though always with a downward tendency, we have already seen to be integral in the scheme of Plotinus. He tells us more of the actual transition from spirit to matter than either Philo or Origen. In the Neoplatonic Trinity the third member, after the One and Spirit, is the Soul. Now the world-soul is in direct contact with the physical universe when it imparts its own nature to the highest phase of the material world, the etherial and rarefied sphere of the outermost heaven, the abode of the fixed stars. If we ask what is the exact operation of the soul, the answer is that it gives form to matter. There is no deliberate act of will. This is expressly denied. By the law of its being soul engenders in its own likeness. What it has known and contemplated in the spiritual world, it reproduces in the physical. Its remembered visions rise again in concrete and material form and the result is great and glorious. Here is an account: "This All that has emerged into life is no amorphous structure, like those lesser forms within it which are born night and day out of the lavishness of its vitality. The Universe is a life organized, effective, complex, all-comprehensive, displaying an unfathomable wisdom. How then can anyone deny that it is a clear image, beautifully formed, of the intellectual divinities? No doubt it is a copy, not original; but that is its very nature; it cannot be at once symbol and reality. But to say that it is an inadequate copy is false; nothing has been left out which a beautiful representation within the physical order could include."

Soul gives form to matter. Matter is receptive. It must be there, in existence, if it is to receive. So, co-existent with spirit, matter would be eternal. This doctrine has considerable support. It is a doubtful point whether matter is eternal in Plato's *Timaeus*. In the periodic cosmic conflagrations of Stoicism the world was reduced by fire to its constituent elements, but the elements remained and were so far eternal. Much discussion has arisen over Philo's teaching on matter. He is not always consistent; indeed, his view may have varied; but Drummond believes Philo did hold the eternity of matter. Photius asserts that Clement taught the same theory, though the statement could hardly be proved from his extant works. Origen alone is clear and plain in maintaining that matter did not always exist. It came into being, and presumably, when the long series of the worlds to be was over and once again the end was as the beginning and God was all in all, matter too with all else would vanish away. We have to reconcile that with his belief that all rational beings, except the Trinity alone, need some kind of bodily organism for their life.

Time, it was usually held, began with the physical world. There were no years before the sun. Relationships, in the purely spiritual world, were timeless and abiding. Such was the relation between the Father and the eternally generated Son, or between the One and Spirit in Neoplatonism. But this principle was sometimes extended to creation. Plotinus held that creation was eternal, matter itself being created, but not in time. Something like this is taught in Philo and in Clement when it is said that the sovereignty and goodness of God were impossible without an object, and that therefore the nature of God involves a universe which consequently must be eternal. Difficulty at once arises when we bring the conception of eternity into relation with the world of sense and physical nature. Where process and succession are so inherent in the scheme, it is difficult to elevate creation to the eternal plane without robbing time of all its reality. I believe modern physics assign to the universe, however vast its duration, both a beginning and an end. There is much to commend this view as preferable to the belief that the universe "is eternal in the sense that it had no temporal beginning and will have no temporal ending." An unending series of cosmic cycles, each exactly like the rest, save for its place in the order, offers little that can satisfy or attract us. We can understand Professor Eddington's reluctance "to see the purpose of the universe banalized by constant repetition".

Thus in regard to the beginning and the end of things, speculation was varied and many views were possible and, when sure data were lacking, probability was an accepted guide. As to the content of the universe, as distinct from its origin and its end, opinion was less divided and traditional views were received with little question. It will be of interest to examine what Alexandrine teachers believed about the heavenly bodies and then about the nature of matter.

Astronomers were at home in Alexandria. It was the only great city in which their especial study could be said to enjoy a national establishment and endowment. One of their number, Eratosthenes, about two centuries B.C., had argued from observation as to the size of the earth and only been some 20 per cent in excess of the actual dimensions in his result. A greater name, that of Hipparchus, meets us half a century later, though he was never more than a visitor in Alexandria and did most of his work in Rhodes. He made a catalogue of 1,080 stars and predicted eclipses and was substantially correct in his calculation of the year. His method was commendable; he collected and recorded observations and made many of his own independently. His work was taken up and developed by Claudius Ptolemæus, an astronomer definitely belonging to Alexandria, whose date in the middle of the second century A.D. makes him a contemporary of Valentinus and perhaps of Clement. What is known from his name as the Ptolemaic astronomy practically remained unchallenged till the time of Copernicus. Ptolemy did little really original work, except in regard to the planets, but he brought traditional views into some sort of unity and deserved his position by his vast diligence both in observation and in his mathematical calculations.

His scheme of the universe, which really went back through Aristotle to Pythagoras, made the earth spherical and located it in the centre of the heavenly spheres, which extended one after the other above and around it. These spheres revolved, each with an independent circular movement of its own, but they were concentric and their common axis ran through the centre of the earth. The fixed stars were attached to the outermost sphere, called οὔρανος, or heaven, because it was the ὅρος or term and boundary of the universe. The etymology is doubtful, the meaning clear. There was nothing beyond, no time, no space, no anything. It is like the modern view of space as finite. In all this Ptolemy did no more than accept current beliefs; they held good as the most probable assumptions. He was more original in his development of the theory of planetary epicycles. This assigned a second and lesser orbit to each planet, in addition to its spherical movement through the heavens. He is said to have obtained results of fair exactitude, much to his credit, if we bear the inadequacy of his instruments in mind.

Living at the centre of things with these vast globes, perhaps of some crystal or more rarefied substance, rising in vast succession one outside the other above him, man might hear through their movements and their mathematical intervals the music of the spheres. So Pythagoras had taught. So imagination might interpret the immensities. The Alexandrines also had their thoughts and imaginations, which were free to wander among the probabilities without the chilling restriction of exact observation.

The sun, the planets, the earth, the stars, were all as they believed living beings. Origen describes the cosmos as a vast and huge animal. The stars he thinks of as living and rational beings. They may sin, as is proved by Job's saying: "The stars are not clean in thy sight." They are endowed with will and desire. He imagines the sun as desiring to be freed from the bondage of corporeal nature and yet as content to run his course in the spirit of voluntary service. He claims, perhaps justly, the support of St. Paul for this view; a world which "groaneth and travaileth in pain together", in which "the earnest expectation of creation" is waiting for a spiritual manifestation, is certainly a universe which strives and desires and is capable of aspiration. In Plotinus Nature contemplates first and then creates. There is consciousness and purpose in the process. The stars too have life and mind and purpose. They are continuously serene, happy in the good they enjoy and the vision before them. Each lives its own free life; each finds its good in its own act. They are willing servants in the cosmic order.

It has been said by Jeans: "We find the universe terrifying because of its vast meaningless distances, terrifying because of its inconceivably long vistas of time which dwarf human history to the twinkling of an eye, terrifying because of our extreme loneliness, and because of the material insignificance of our home in space—a millionth part of a grain of sand out of all the sea-sand in the world. But above all else, we find the universe terrifying because it appears to be indifferent to life like our own; emotion, ambition and achievement, art and religion all seem equally foreign to its plan. Perhaps indeed we ought to say it appears to be actively hostile to life like our own."

With such a verdict we may contrast the views of an earlier day, when will and purpose and reason and ideal aims, all the qualities we assign to human nature at its best, were without hesitation ascribed to other forms of being beside "Homo Sapiens". This teaching may have been a survival of animism or unconsciously anthropomorphic. At least it has still this value that it raises for us the question whether consciousness or even personality may not be more widely existent in the universe than we commonly suppose. We have banished even the angels. In Alexandria they believed in communion with the stars.

The general scheme of cosmic order with the central earth and the revolving spheres is accepted by the Alexandrines from tradition. But within this scheme there was much opportunity for speculation. Here are one or two examples.

There is interest in Philo's insistence upon the

essential unity of the world. The universe is a whole, an order. Its parts are associated by a certain communion and sympathy. Invisible bonds unite the outermost heaven with the earth we know, and it is their action which prevents the cosmos falling asunder in dissolution. This is very like the essentially Hellenic view found in St. Paul's statement that in him, in the Son, all things consist, τὰ πάντα ἐν αὐτῷ συνέστηκε, find their unity, which is pure Logos doctrine, though St. Paul does not use the term. In Philo's view Moses and the Chaldeans, who were the pioneers in the study of the stars, were agreed in believing that the heavens and the earth were in intimate relationship; there was an organic harmony in the universe wherein every part and every element, the great and the small together, the flowing stream, no less than the fixed stars, had all their proper place and function. Those elements which were individually and particularly imperfect were perfect when seen in relation to the whole. This was a common theory with the Stoics and got over many difficulties. As an order or a unity the whole was good, and Philo finds the cosmos so complete that it leaves neither room nor necessity for any other world. Here his successors did not follow him, and he was obviously parting company with the Stoics. There was a single cosmos as there was a single Creator. It is no long series of system after system, world after world, but a universe of solitary splendour once created but indissoluble and incorruptible, originating in time but continuing through all eternity, a cosmos that is veritably single, sole and one.

Here is a characteristic idea from Origen. The astronomical conception of sphere beyond sphere, globe outside globe, he brings into connection with the saying of the Lord: "In my Father's house are many mansions." And Origen, blending things physical with things spiritual after his wont, pictures the ascent of the pure soul as it passes from orb to orb in the successive stages, discovering in each the reason of that circle's particular mode and operation, till at last the outer sphere of the fixed stars is attained and the ascended soul learns why this or that particular star has its special position, its own size, its proper distance from the other stars and how not one of these items could have been other than it is without the totality of the whole order suffering influence and change. This sense of the exactness and the intimate connection of nature's order almost anticipates the modern scientific view, and we get things in Clement of the same kind. But even the stars and the revolutions of the spheres do not bring the soul's experience to an end. They are the last stage, the final phase of knowledge, in the world of things seen and physical; beyond lies the world invisible, spiritual, indescribable. So do the saints who are pure in heart pass from the final stage of this material universe into the lowest grade of the world beyond. "Whether in the body or whether out of the body," with Paul, "I cannot tell." In any case for Origen the transition seemed normal, natural, with nothing painful, nothing violent.

Here again is the reason Plotinus gives for the revolution of the heavens. There must be movement in the spheres, for in bodily things if there is no movement there is no life. So the Cosmos, being a living thing, must have movement. But the natural movement of body is straight on. Now the cosmos is a thing of body. Within it the constituent element of the heavens is fire, possibly solidified with a slight admixture of earth, but even fire moves naturally in a straight line. But if the stars moved for ever in a direct motion, onwards, they would be flung outside the universe, which could not be. But the soul also has its movement, and the natural movement of the soul Plotinus conceives as circular. It revolves. In this Soul imitates Mind or Spirit. Now the action of the cosmic soul within the bodily cosmos is to restrain or deflect the body from its normal straight-onwards motion into a curve. There is the additional consideration that when a body has moved in a direct line into its destined place, there it comes to rest. Thus a second cause operates to arrest the straight-on course of the cosmos. Being in its destined position and so losing its outward momentum, being also impelled by the action of the cosmic soul within it to a curved motion, it so arrives at a pure circuit. It does not advance. It revolves. There is motion, but it is circular, on its axis. The value of this piece of speculation for Plotinus is that it enables him to combine the conceptions of motion and rest. The thing which revolves upon itself is in action and yet stationary. In a figure permanence and change are so brought into unity. That is why the universe, circling as it does, is at the same time at rest. This solution of a problem was sufficient for its age. For us its interest lies in the fusion of physical and spiritual conceptions.

The spheres and orbits of the planets, as they recede from the central earth, come in the following order, as Philo tells us. First is that of the Moon: lowest, nearest, close to the air. Then follow Venus and Mercury, and after, in the central position, the Sun. Beyond the sun are Jupiter, Mars, Saturn. The sun and moon were included with the five planets and so make the total of seven. And Venus is regarded as nearer to the earth than Mercury. The lowest orbit, that of the moon, was a recognized boundary line. Aristotle had placed there the limit of the operation of providence. Beyond this line existences in the scheme of Plotinus were eternal. The sun and the stars did not suffer change and growth. But below this boundary all physical nature was subject to birth and growth and decay and death. The individual came and departed. Only type and form were permanent. The same boundary separated the celestial from the sub-celestial. Fire, too, with its admixture of earthly substance, could only rise to the level of the lunar orbit. Beyond, flame was of purer and more etherial nature. It is all part of a fairly coherent scheme, as irreconcilable as the first chapters of Genesis with modern knowledge, but the scheme had its dignity and completeness and had regard for facts as far as they were understood. Origen, for example, was quite aware of the causes which produce an eclipse, and can discuss in the temper of the true enquirer the reasons for the darkness at the crucifixion.

A subject much under discussion was the influence of the stars upon human life. From early times there had been recognized relations between the heavenly bodies and the weather. Sun, moon, and stars had been observed in connection with the sowing and the gathering of the crops. This natural and reasonable theory passed beyond the assured area of observation and was developed by the Chaldeans into planetary lore and all the elaborations of astrological speculation. The Greeks, it has been said, gave to Chaldean and Egyptian astrology "the precision and the finish and the false lustre of a scientific method". For a century before Christ and long after, the eastern star-readers had been an influential tribe, repeatedly driven from Rome but consulted even by the very emperors who expelled them. Tiberius and Nero, the curious Hadrian and the severe Marcus, all recognized and used the science of the stars. Its professors were numerous in Alexandria. The vogue and wide influence of this superstition gave it an importance which could not be ignored. Astral lore was not wholly rejected by our Platonists. For Christian writers, for Origen and for Tertullian, there was the difficulty of the story of the Magi. The fathers might distinguish as they would the New Testament narrative from the assertions and claims of the astrologers; in any case the star's guidance of the Wise Men could not be denied. Nor is Plotinus prepared to ignore the stars. The universe is too intimately related to admit of their isolation. "Our personality is bound up with the stars." And there is a curious similarity here between Christianity and Neoplatonism. Both explicitly admit that the stars indicate events. The heavenly bodies announce the future. It is their office to predict what is to come. Writers of both schools think of the heavens as a book which may be read. "We may think of the stars," says Plotinus, "as letters perpetually being described on the heavens." And for Origen when the heavens "shall be folded up like a book" it will be because all that was written therein has been fulfilled. The position is clear; coming events are foretold by the stars.

But prediction is not causation. The stars indicate what they do not determine. No horoscope compels a man to his fate. We are not rich or poor, good or bad, miserable or happy, because this or that planet was dominant at the hour of our birth. Signs ordained to be tokens do not hinder our free action. The objection to astrology is that its fatalism robs man of moral liberty. The old question whether Peter was free not to deny his Lord after Jesus had predicted that he would do so, suggests itself as a parallel to the position frequently asserted by Origen that the future is known and yet open. So was it said of the stars that they indicate but they do not control. Plotinus devotes a long Tractate to this discussion.

The æther and the stars were the highest, most rarefied, most nearly spiritual form of physical being. We shall turn now to the other end of the scale and consider its lowest grade. The Greeks called this ὕλη; it is our matter.

THE UNIVERSE

The first point to note is that for the Platonists, who in this point are definitely irreconcilable with the Stoics, matter was not material. It was an abstraction. It was the *substratum* of things, itself indeterminate and without qualities, shapeless, formless, without mass, or extension, purely passive, purely receptive, that which is left when every quality that can be assigned to things has been stripped away. When you say a thing is square or white or beautiful or desirable or useful you attribute to it characteristics, determined features, actuality, form. What receives or possesses all these is matter. It is like the "substance" which in later philosophy was distinguished from all its "accidents". Logically matter is prior to form. Actually it never exists without form; it is indeed "τὸ μὴ ὄν", the thing that, as yet, without form, is non-existent.

This abstraction, matter, is the substratum of all actual being. Its function is to render a cosmos possible, it is the necessary basis upon which cosmic order is built up. It has its place in the spiritual as in the physical world. Plotinus speaks of it as *There* as well as *Here*. Origen says the Holy Spirit supplies the material out of which the gifts and grace of God are made. It is the stuff of all things. It has its place in the scheme of the *Timaeus*, perhaps in that of the book of Genesis. And it is as little material, in our sense of the term, as the atoms of modern scientific theory. It is curious how the ancient process of abstract thought and the modern development of mathematical physics have reached so closely similar a result.

Of this ὕλη, matter, substratum of being, you may say the best as you may say the worst. The Alexandrines did both, but more especially the latter. In praise of matter, or at least to its credit, might be urged that it made possible all the variety and beauty of the physical universe. No star shone, no flower bloomed without it. By its passive co-operation all forms and ideas came into actuality, and the soul of the world would have been impotent without its aid. It was sufficient and did not fail in its cosmic function. Matter, Philo said, was exactly adequate for the fabrication of this glorious world. Equally with the Logos, the highest of the subordinate spiritual agencies, matter in its humbler place might claim to be the servant of God in creation. In the lower world through its wonderful elasticity it is "ready to go here, there, and everywhere". In the higher, beyond the operation of change, divine matter has a life defined and spiritual, in permanent association with form in its highest mode.

But the common account was adverse and perhaps unfair. The "excessive recoil from materialism", which Edward Caird lays to the charge of the Alexandrines, is seen inevitably in their account of ὕλη. Matter is contrasted more often than associated with form. It is the lowest constituent. It limits the spirit. It beguiles the soul that enters into it. It drags its spiritual visitor down to lower levels and even sinks it in the mud. Constantly the epithets applied to it are such terms as lifeless, shapeless, corruptible, base, despicable, shifting, defective. It is classed with vice and corruption. At best it is devoid in its own nature of all good. More often it is the positive cause of evil, restricting ideals, thwarting the purpose of the artificer, occasioning sin. We may recall all that St. Paul had to say about the flesh wherein "dwelleth no good thing", or Virgil's line:

> Quantum non noxia tardant
> Corpora.

Origen describes matter as the devil's mistress. For Plotinus matter is "utter destitution of sense, of virtue, of beauty, of pattern, of ideal principle, of quality. This is surely ugliness, utter disgracefulness, unredeemed evil".

Yet, except the Gnostics, these Platonists were in the long run optimists, on the side of the angels. All evil in the cosmos was partial, and what in part was evil might be for the advantage of the whole. It had been claimed in Alexandria that "the generative powers of the world are healthsome", and that "even if we sin, we are thine". Perhaps evil, as Origen thought, was only the rubbish left around the building when the work was done and the building itself was glorious. Out of lower material the higher power, whether the Christian Logos, or the Neoplatonic Soul, or the Old Testament Wisdom, could fashion first the four elements, earth, air, water, fire, and then in ascending differentiation, up and up the scale of being, the varied forms of terrestial and super-terrestial life. Nor, like the sombre Lucretius, did the Platonists arrest their thoughts at the confines of space, for beyond the "flammantia mœnia mundi" was the spirit world, of which this universe was but a defective copy. Into this transition was possible. The natural passed over to the spiritual, the corruptible into the incorruptible. So was creation redeemed and justified and the *Here* found compatible with the *There*. From densest matter to the purest star the attractive power of the ultimately good drew nature towards itself.

With all the teachers of this school it is an accepted doctrine that the order of the world is regulated by Providence. The power which originated also ordered and sustained. The cosmos is permeated by a controlling and directive agency which operates in the whole mass and in its smallest parts. This principle is asserted with emphasis, just because it was frequently challenged. It was indeed at this period one main criterion of philosophy. Schools which admitted Providence were commendable; schools which denied it were discredited and were deserving not only of reasoned opposition but also of many abusive epithets. The whole attitude of the Platonists towards the Epicureans, who frankly denied Providence, was that they were scandalous and disreputable people, who were guilty philosophically of mortal sin. The Platonists did not use the same language in regard to Aristotle and the Peripatetics, but at least their silence on so important a doctrine was lamentable and almost impious. On the other hand it was a common point between the Alexandrines and Stoicism. All the Stoic masters had asserted Providence. According to Zeno it was providence which sustained the cosmos. The belief indeed was only another aspect of their doctrine of an immanent God. And this common article of faith appears in the book of Wisdom, where all things are in the divine order, and nothing is beyond God's watchful superintending care. For Philo children and obscure persons equally with the totality of the cosmic scheme are under the same beneficent regulation. And at the root of Clement's happy optimism lies the same conviction, which as De Faye notes is not so much with Clement a philosophical tenet as a religious faith, for God's people are under the care of a Good Shepherd, and the teaching of the Prophets and the redemptive work of the Saviour alike evidence the unseen directive purpose and the all-pervading love. The references in Origen to providence, πρόνοια, are numerous. Its action was so plain you could almost see it; it was σχεδὸν αἰσθητή. And Plotinus will allow no domination either to atoms or to circumstances. Providence permeates the Cosmos from first to last. He compares providence to a general, and "When the mighty general is in question whose power extends over all that is, what can pass unordered, what can fail to fit into the plan?"

Now this is all very assured, very serene. We are in the best possible of worlds. But awkward questions could not always be avoided and some unpleasant facts were too obvious to be ignored. On two grounds the belief in providence was challenged and we may note both the objections and the answers; we still have to recognize the force of the objections and the limitations of the answers.

First, it was urged that the universe was not wholly good. Pain and suffering were only too plentiful. Evil beasts devoured their helpless prey. Men slaughtered one another in battle. Tempests shattered the handiwork of man. Earthquakes destroyed his security. The bite of poisonous serpents brought his end. They did not know so well as we do how much cruelty underlies the pleasant exterior of nature, but they knew enough to realize the force of the question, whether all was really very good. Moreover, when from the order of nature the mind passed to the conditions of human life and saw the apparent disregard of merit, the bad in control, the good in slavery, Socrates drinking the hemlock and Jesus crucified and Christian martyrs perishing without any intervention or deliverance, all the old problems of the prosperity of the wicked and the sufferings of the righteous man recurring, just as they had confronted the Psalmists and challenged God himself in the book of Job, it becomes possible to understand the concern felt by Origen when Celsus anticipated Carlyle's question and asked: "If God and Providence are as you say, why do they not set things right?" That was one difficulty. The second was this: If providence orders all, what becomes of human freedom? Are men agents or only instruments? Have you room in your scheme both for an all-ruling providence and for a human will? Only in outline can we indicate the way these difficulties were met.

Sometimes, like the Stoics, the Alexandrines

said no real evil could befall the good, and that poverty or disease did not involve unhappiness. Conversely it was urged that the wicked man was never truly happy. Or it was maintained, especially by Neoplatonists, that providence aimed at the good of the whole and that what seemed evil in particular was beneficial in the wider view. In a good play there may be a bad character, and the nature of the universe seems to demand such contraries. Again the fall of Jerusalem and the death of the Lord, apparently evil when seen in isolation, were really essential elements in a divine economy. Or suffering was punishment, and all punishment was remedial and educative. Often our unhappiness in one life is due to our own action in a previous state of existence. This is common doctrine to Origen and Plotinus. What befalls us here is deserved discipline intended only for our good. Or the adjustment is found not in the past but in the future. "The souls of the righteous are in the hands of God," and what men accounted their hurt here has worked out to their immortal gain. Here a little chastening, there the great good. If there are violent forces in nature, they may really purify, just as states need their executioners. Origen suggests that disasters occur because of the lowered vitality of the universe; nature fails as the human body fails. Or it was possible to fall back upon the teaching of the *Timaeus* which regarded the Cosmos as springing from the combination of Reason and Necessity. Reason and therefore providence could not claim absolute control. Necessity was always a limit. The cosmos was a thing of mixture and more than was possible must not be demanded even of a glorious and wonderful universe. In regard to human freedom its most unhesitating defender is Origen; αἰτία ἑλομένου is his constant principle. He finds the cause of all evil, cosmic or individual-human, in wrong choice. Man sins by will, as the devil and other higher cosmic powers had sinned and vitiated the universe at an earlier stage. Plotinus has two interesting Tractates on Providence and is far more qualified in his view. He tries to reconcile man's agency with this all-pervading, all-determining power. And he evidently finds the reconciliation difficult, as we all do. Perhaps he may be said to approximate to the position of St. Paul who said man should work out his own salvation because it was God who worked within him. Such in outline were the available resources of the Platonists when they set about to justify providence and find in one quarter or another explanation for admitted evil. They hardly achieved their task with finality, but they did no worse than many other champions of the same cause.

To what extent did the Alexandrines appreciate the Beauty of the universe? Can they be said to have ranked, as we do, the Beautiful with the Good and the True? It was a frequent assertion of Stoicism that through the wonder and beauty of the cosmic order man first came to believe in God. We have the same teaching in Philo. The outward senses are as windows and through them we behold the indescribable order and harmony of the world and are led in thought from creation to the Creator. To each created thing, says Clement, its own peculiar beauty has been assigned He devotes a chapter in the *Pædagogus* to the "True Beauty", which is inward, of the soul. Plotinus has much to say on this subject, and urges that there is more in beauty than mere symmetry and proportion. He is impatient with the Gnostics, who were indifferent to beauty in nature and depreciated the visible order of the world after their manner. Flame and gold and colour and the stars were all arresting instances of beauty. The Platonists would have allowed the saying of Ecclesiastes that God "hath made every thing beautiful in its time".

And yet they fail to recognize æsthetic value at its true worth. For the very term *æsthetic* implies an activity of sense and the Platonists were notoriously suspicious of all that belonged to that domain. Sensuous beauty was associated with the body and the body was the prison and impediment of the soul. Moreover, sun, moon, stars, had of old been worshipped by the heathen and so robbed the Creator of his due, and even in the second century the sun-worship of Mithra was a serious rival to Christianity. Hence comes a certain restraint in the praise which Philo and the Christians would bestow upon nature's beauty. The variety and the movement of the universe are large elements in its æsthetic value, but the Platonists suspected change and multiplicity, and sought to find permanent and abiding beauty that should be independent of the domain of sense. So once again they lead us to the higher world of the spirit where ideal Beauty is associated with the Real and the Good. Clement's Gnostic finds no satisfaction in the human form. Plotinus says the soul must ignore what comes through sight and hearing, it must mount higher, "leaving sense to its own low place". We are to seek beauty outside of sense, for natural beauty holds us down. The true lover of beauty will "turn away for ever from the natural beauty that once made his joy". Real beauty belongs to the spiritual world. There we may have vision which surpasses in its wonder the beauty of evening and of dawn. In our quest we must ascend again towards the good, we must "flee to the beloved fatherland". Sunset and moonlight and the waters and the sculptor's art must interest us no longer. Beauty's seat is *There*.

Such idealism is excessive. The visible world has higher value. Even Neoplatonism taught that what is *There* is *Here*. When Beauty is wholly spiritualized, its æsthetic value is practically ignored. Plato taught in the *Phædrus* that beauty more than any other ideal form reaches us directly because it comes to us through sight, the clearest of all the bodily senses. Certainly, if Goodness, Truth and Beauty are alike our ultimate values and the highest attributes of God, the manifestation of the divine in beauty is the purest and least contaminated by alien elements of all the three. For goodness is ever qualified by defect or actual evil, and truth is with difficulty extracted from the mass of uncertainties and error, whereas the beauty of the universe is a direct and unspoiled expression of the divine, and comes to us without our toil or pain and free from the strife and contest which pervade the moral and intellectual spheres. So perhaps the Alexandrines failed to recognize the æsthetic value of the visible universe. Their appreciation falls far below that of the hundred and fourth Psalm, far below that of Jesus who said: "Consider the lilies."

So in an earlier age did those who followed in the way of Plato look out upon the visible universe.

If we attempt to compare their attitude and estimate with our own, many contrasts are at once plain. What has been called the "climate of opinion" is different. Methods of enquiry and standards of evidence are so changed as to be hardly comparable. Our thoughts on nature are restrained by experiment and observation. Our way is that of induction; the ancients reasoned from above. The apparatus and instruments of scientific enquiry have at once enlarged and determined our knowledge. Our small planet is no longer the centre of the universe. The authority of great teachers or great discoverers closes for us no questions. And we are far more conscious of the remoteness of finality in our interpretation of the visible world. The general character of these contrasts may perhaps be summarized under two heads.

First, we are plainly much more interested in physical nature for its own sake than the Alexandrines were. Nor is it sufficient to say that this is naturally so because we know more about it. We set a higher value on the lower approach to reality and have wholly abandoned the depreciatory estimate of material things. Philosophy and theology have in large measure given place to science and no one now questions the right of science to omit and ignore, though not to deny, spiritual values which do not hold good within the scientific area. Mystics, like Plotinus, have experienced contact with reality in the mystic manner by escaping from the things of sense. But reality is one, and the enquirer who after years of toil and quest discovers new truth in a laboratory may be said to share the mystic's experience by a different method of approach. For the Platonists the real things, τὰ ὄντα, belonged to the spiritual world. The lower, concrete visible world so became a copy, an imperfect reproduction of the ideal. Time could only imitate eternity. The actual Jerusalem was a poor place. Only the Jerusalem that was above or the πολίτεια that was laid up as a pattern in the heavens were really worth loving as the homes of spirits that are free. The scheme was dualistic, this characteristic varying in degree but always so felt and operative as to leave only secondary value to the physical universe. From this dualistic view we have long moved away. The world is one. The scientific interest has its claim in company with the moral and the religious. We are told that mechanistic theories are no longer dominant in physical enquiry and that we need no longer fear that the advance of knowledge may leave us with a universe that has no soul. That is gain and reassurance. But at least the long dominance of mechanism has taught us, at whatever cost of abstraction, to see the importance of physical nature, to apprehend more of the wonder of its ways, and to feel how reality, τὰ ὄντα, are not only *There* but also *Here*. Allow, in the common phrase, that it "takes all sorts to make a world", that appearance must be admitted as well as reality, that the new science seems likely to dematerialize matter, that criteria of quality must be allowed as well as those of quantity, it will still remain that physical nature is for us in our day immensely interesting, and that on its own account. In this we differ from the Alexandrines. We must not condemn them for their indifference. They had their own message and they lived in their own day. But let us recognize our gain.

Secondly, the proportions of Permanence and Change in physical nature are different when we compare our view with that of Alexandria. Both elements are there, for the very idea of change implies something which holds the two elements in a succession together and gives unity to the otherwise wholly unconnected items. There were philosophers, followers of Heraclitus, who held that all was in constant flux, πάντα ῥεῖ, and who were known as οἱ ῥέοντες, and there was the dictum that you cannot step into the same river twice. But it is the same person who tries to step in; otherwise the saying has no point. The Platonists were of another type; what is eternal and unchanging is prominent in their scheme. Conditions in the spiritual world are permanent and abiding. The Idea of the Good knows no variation. The fundamental contrast is between what is and what comes into being and passes out of it. They view the whole process of nature against a background of unalterable reality. Behind the shifting seasons and the wandering planets we have the Logos, eternally generated, the universe created but not in time, the revolving movement of the heavens which is compatible with abiding rest. Even within the physical visible range of being there were incorruptible, unaltering elements. The outer stars knew no change. Material substance could be so pure as to be immortal. Relatively the permanent was important, the changing less in extent and value.

Contrast the universe of modern science. The very uniformity of Nature is called in question. What seems solid is in violent motion. Types as well as individuals come and go. Evolution, radiation, light-waves, attraction, nature's modes of operation, the dying sun—in a word all the familiar terminology of science is saturated with the conception of change. Space and time alike seem full of process. Men of science admit the innate hunger for permanence in our minds, but little of

THE UNIVERSE 131

objective value in nature seems left to satisfy the demand. Even the laws of nature have lost something of their inviolable rigidity. For a world controlled in great and small by a divine Logos we have a world in which evolution, perhaps without prior intention, creates instinctively as it goes upon its way. We are approximating intellectually to the condition of πάντα ῥεῖ. We may have faith that in one way or another the permanent and the eternal will be saved. But in any case they bulk less largely in our outlook upon physical nature than they did when men watched the nightly stars from the garden of the Museum in Alexandria.

Yet if there are differences between their way and ours, there are also points of contact, and even in regard to nature we may wish to see the world in some respects as they did. By their own methods, which are not ours, they combined spiritual with material being, and if they sometimes separated God and nature by too sharp a division, at least they knew that both were there. Bigg says of Clement and Origen that almost alone they strove to reconcile the revelation of God in Jesus with the older revelation of God in nature. If we in our day have tried to rest satisfied with a mechanical theory of the universe and found it wanting, that is only to say that for us as for the Alexandrines the spiritual element must be included in any complete account of the universe, that love and purpose have to be recognized as well as weight and numbers.

Once again in physical nature they saw a copy and a manifestation of a reality that was higher and unseen. Just as in Scripture through allegory they discovered an inner significance, so in creation invisible things were made plain through visible. Plotinus, agreeing with an earlier Platonist, Maximus of Tyre, said that "All teems with symbol." The wise man is the man who in any one thing can read another. So have modern poets, especially Wordsworth, found spiritual significance in nature, and from quite another standpoint it has been said: "We are dealing in physics with a symbolic world." The conviction of a something more behind phenomena may be a point of contact between an ancient and the modern world.

Finally they had the gift of wonder. In their way they felt the universe was glorious and admirable. Living in the latter days of a declining civilization they still could share the joy experienced by the Homeric shepherd when he saw the stars come out at night. And it is well indeed for us if our increased knowledge of Nature does not rob us of the power to admire the majesty, the variety, the mystery and the inexpressible beauty of her ways.

LECTURE IV

MAN

WE shall consider in this concluding lecture the views of the Alexandrine teachers on the nature of man. Let us begin with the admission that they were in no sense humanists. Man is not the centre of their interest, nor indeed is his life here and now in this world the principal stage in his career. He is interesting for his destiny rather than for his achievements. His three score years and ten are brief indeed in comparison with the long succession of the ages, and his personality is somewhat dwarfed by comparison with the higher spiritual powers whose activities are on the cosmic scale. He is akin to them indeed, but we cannot wholly ignore the factor of size and grandeur and permanence in our comparison, so that the microcosm is patently inferior to the macrocosm. The stars were living, rational, moral beings, and it was the sight of the heavens which prompted the Psalmist's question: "What is man that thou art mindful of him?" We are a long way from Hamlet's estimate: "What a piece of work is a man!" Over all that the Alexandrines said and thought about him there rests the sense that he is a fallen creature, a stranger wandering in a country which is not his own. The Alexandrines were Platonists and their real loyalty is given to the city in the heavens. Perhaps without surrendering this they might have allowed more value to the sane conclusion of Aristotle's *Ethics* that the true good for human nature is discoverable in the exercise of its varied faculties at their best, κατ' ἀρετήν, with a real sense of value in what is present and what is possible.

What is man's origin? How does he come here? Plainly man is a composite creature, body and soul, or perhaps a trinity, as St. Paul spoke of his body, soul and spirit. The origin of the human body is to us a question of fascinating interest. Man's place in physical nature, since Darwin and Huxley, has been more and more determined, and religious people are no longer troubled by what science has to tell them of their probable physical ancestry. In Alexandria the doctors knew a great deal about the human body. Eighty-three works of Galen, mostly medical, still survive. The body had its different elements, its hot and cold, its moist and dry, and a right balance and proportion of these constituents was a main factor in good health. Clement, no doubt, had friends among the doctors, for here and there in his discursive writings we find sections on medical subjects which betray interest and familiarity. He knew, for example, what was thought in the schools on the ante-natal processes. Origen, too, had met doctors who explained by normal physical action conditions more generally attributed to demoniacal possession. But their views of the body were of course static rather than evolutionary, so that it was accepted as an organism with functions and members, of whose original making it was enough to say that "the Lord God formed man out of the dust of the ground", or just that it was "matter", ὕλη, the inferior element, but a necessary condition for the life of rational beings or at least for some of them.

But in the origin of the other element, the soul, the Alexandrines were more interested. Origen says that there were three possible theories on the subject. Either the soul came by creation, so that a new soul came into being for every body, or the soul came by what we should term heredity, which is the traducianist explanation and implies that along with the physical element spiritual qualities also came from parent to child, on which modern Eugenists have so much to say. Thirdly was the account that rested upon the supposition of pre-existence; the soul came into the body *ab extra*, having lived earlier lives and bringing with it the qualities and a nature which it had acquired by its own conduct. There is an obvious similarity between this theory and the Buddhist doctrine of "Karma". It is an unsettled question whether on this point eastern and western doctrine arose independently, by a parallel growth, or whether they had a common source.

Between these different explanations opinions varied. Clement alone leaves us in no doubt that he believed each soul existed by separate creation; "God made us; we did not pre-exist. Had we pre-existed we should have known where we had been and how and why we came here. If we did not pre-exist, God alone is responsible for our birth." And all his references to Gnostic reincarnation are adverse. Nor has he anything to say for Platonic recollection, $\dot{\alpha}\nu\dot{\alpha}\mu\nu\eta\sigma\iota\varsigma$. On this point Clement's position is clear and defined.

Philo before him had been less sure. As so often Philo had learned something from Plato and something from the Scriptures, and the two elements remain in his teaching unreconciled. There are passages in which he fully accepts in Plato's way the independent existence of the soul. The soul was either etherial or wholly uncorporeal in nature; in either case it descended into the body from its own place and sphere. But in other passages the account in Genesis is accepted in its literal sense. God breathed into man the breath of life. This, it seems, was his real view. Drummond thinks his adoption of Platonic pre-existence may have been only a passing phase in his strangely blended speculation. If Philo did suppose "that the concrete and individual mind had descended into the body from the choir of aerial souls, he makes no use of this supposition, but proceeds as though each man began his mental history with his birth." On the whole then we may associate Philo with Clement as holding that each soul comes into being by a separate creative act.

But the Gnostics, Origen, Plotinus, and even the earlier book of Wisdom, teach the advent of the soul, not its creation. "I was a goodly child and a good soul fell to my lot; nay rather, being good, I came into a body undefiled." The independent and prior existence of the soul is clearly implied. We have a more detailed account of the soul's descent to bodily conditions in the notices given us of the system of Basilides. The soul in this Gnostic theory dwells in the upper heaven which is fixed and immobile. Prompted by desire the soul seeks a less immaterial existence, first clothing itself with an etherial envelope of rarefied tenuity, then little by little acquiring more weight and solidity till it comes down to the planetary spheres in each of which it loses something of its pure spirituality. In the sphere of Saturn it gains intelligence, in that of Jupiter activity; Mars and Venus give it courage and desire, Mercury speech, the Moon growth. So when it reaches earth it is fully adapted to wear its coat of clay and it remains united to the earthly body till, with death, the hour arrives for its return journey. There is a certain dramatic completeness in this poetic scheme, its notable feature, as with the Paradise story, being the evil of desire.

The soul with Origen also pre-exists. Originally God created a number, large but definite, of rational natures, all free, all equal. By their acts of choice they rose or fell in the spiritual scale and in the whole long process of many ages, many worlds, each soul is born into just that body which it has deserved and which will afford it the best opportunities of discipline and development. "I loved Jacob and I hated Esau," is a hard saying, but the difficulty vanishes if their different fortunes are due to their lives in an earlier world. The soul that is united to a human body has really made itself, and there is no great teacher who has laid so terrible a weight of responsibility upon man's free will as Origen.

In this point he is more definite than Plotinus, who recognizes more than one explanation of the soul's incarnation. Once, he tells us in an interesting reminiscence, that he had come down from a mood of contemplation to a more discursive phase of thought, and the change had forced upon him the question: How did any soul enter any body? He devotes a whole tractate to the answer, which is not so much final as suggestive. The soul descends into the body because of the necessity that lower forms of existence should come into being, or because itself it desired to have this experience, even at times deserting its higher loyalty. Or again the soul may have been sent; it comes on a mission, by a divine sowing. Or it comes to care for lower things, to order, to administer and rule. Perhaps its own audacity has caused its fall into material conditions. Perhaps it comes because the experience of this lower life will result in later advantage; pain is gain, $\pi\alpha\theta\epsilon\hat{\iota}\nu\ \mu\alpha\theta\epsilon\hat{\iota}\nu$. Thus a variety of causes may have brought us here. Perhaps when we consider the origin of the individual in relation to the whole scheme of the universe as Neoplatonism understood it, we must find the dominant factor not in an individual will or in a divine purpose but in the inherent nature of things, in the tendency of being to overflow or generate in the downward sweep from unity to multiplicity. So the world-soul, the lowest member of the trinity, is differentiated into a manifold of individuals, the one becomes the many, and man finds himself in the middle place linked upwards to the *anima mundi*, downwards to the beasts that perish and to the matter which resists and degrades, and to the evil which in reality is not his own and yet from which in practice here he is never free.

From the modern standpoint it is surprising that the Alexandrines make so little use of the traducianist theory of the soul's origin; as we say, of heredity. Whatever may be said in regard to the vexed question of the transmission of acquired qualities, the main fact of inherited character and temperament, even if all due allowance be made for environmental influence, is sufficiently clear. And in the ancient world the Stoics were quite aware of this. It accorded with their theories of the corporeal nature of the soul. If physical process explained the likeness of bodily features between parent and child, should not the same process account for the equally obvious likeness of moral disposition and spiritual qualities? It was no doubt their Platonist dislike of such an explanation that made the Alexandrines avoid the doctrine of physical heredity. They refused to explain the cosmos by atoms and they equally refused to explain the individual by "cells", or by whatever was the equivalent of cells, στοιχεῖα probably, in the medical schools of their day. Once again their reaction from materialism carried them too far.

So, body and soul, man comes into being, a

composite creature, a wanderer between two worlds, God's image stamped on clay. And yet our arrival here is no matter for unqualified gratitude. "Trailing clouds of glory do we come." Plotinus at any rate would have admitted Wordsworth's belief. But it is a descent. The soul comes down. Birth is a fall. We are prisoners and captives. Life is a dungeon, at best a school away from home. It is not "Unto us a child is born, unto us a son is given." There is no "joy that a man is born into the world". We do not "bless thee for our creation". Clement indeed, the optimist of his company, can write with enthusiasm on home life and children and count *genesis* a gain. But even Clement had his moments of disillusionment and Origen and Plotinus are more outspoken on the cost and loss of our sojourn here. Individual souls, living in the spiritual world, make the downward journey and this is how Plotinus describes it: "There comes a stage at which they descend from the universal to become partial and self-centred; in a weary desire of standing apart they find their way, each to a place of its very own. This state long maintained, the soul is a deserter from the All; its differentiation has severed it; its vision is no longer set in the intellectual or spiritual; it is a partial thing, isolated, weakened, full of care, intent upon the fragment; severed from the whole, it nestles in one form of being, for this it abandons all else, entering into and caring only for the unit, for a thing buffeted about by a worldful of things; thus it has drifted away from the universal and by an actual presence it administers the particular; it is caught into contact now, and tends to the outer to which it has become present and into whose depths it henceforth sinks far." We wonder how, after writing this, Plotinus could scold the Gnostics for their pessimism.

A like sentiment underlies a passage in Origen, where he quaintly remarks that only bad men celebrate their birthdays. Pharaoh did so in the Old Testament and Herod in the New. But the saints, Jeremiah for instance and Job, if Job was a saint, are far from such rejoicing and even curse the day of their birth. Why should the law prescribe purification for a woman after childbirth, and why should the Church order baptism of infants for the remission of sins, if birth were not in some way associated with evil? The ascetic strain is evident. We are on the road that led to monasteries and convents and the hermit's cell. The soul had descended. Let it shun the world and all its evil and keep itself as uncontaminated as may be, till the time comes for its return. The estimate of life implied is surely very different from the teaching of Jesus on service and stewardship and the right use of this world's goods. Such other-worldliness is not unqualified. The Alexandrines have something to say on the other side. But on the whole the soul of man has come down. The body is limitation rather than medium and opportunity.

What these teachers thought about man's origin we have seen. Their hopes and speculation as to his ultimate destiny we shall consider later. Meantime between our arrival here and our passing hence there is, here and now, this present life. More and more in the modern world it claims the large share in our interest, and yet indeed this is an old story: "They eat, they drank, they bought, they sold, they builded, they planted, they married and were given in marriage." "Quicquid agunt homines, votum, timor, ira, voluptas." The crowds grow denser in the market of Vanity Fair. We wish at times the Alexandrines had said little more about this normal life of humanity, but they think less of earth than they do of heaven and are definitely more interested in the past and future than in the present.

Thus when we come to investigate their account of man we find little attention given to his economic and political activities. Slave labour and the *Pax Romana* no doubt contributed to this restriction of interest. The Romans managed their empire reasonably well, and Egypt was important enough to secure its particular share in Cæsar's attention. The daily routine went on; the philosophers did not notice it. Such things as business enterprise or statesmanship or all that we denote by the "social question" did not come within their range. The life of action was in no sense their concern.

Incidentally, however, they notice from time to time the material conditions of existence. It is in the order of Providence that the earth should bring forth crops for the use of man and that the animals should minister to his needs. Stoics had much to say on this topic. Origen joins issue with Celsus, who had claimed superiority for the animals, asserting that many animals could prey on man instead of being his prey, that bees and ants had much to teach us in civilization and progress, and that the elephant was more reliable in the matter of keeping an oath. Philo at an earlier date had pointed out that man had no superiority over the other animals in his physical outfit, for the eagle was more sharp-sighted, the ass had better hearing, the dog a keener scent. The real advantage of the human kind lay in man's spiritual nature. He might be the lowest of rational beings, still man had reason and not only sense and instinct, therefore it was in the divine order that plants and animals should minister to his needs.

In the order of creation as given in the book of Genesis man was created last, so that every preparation for his minor needs might be already made in nature. The ample supplies of unspoiled Eden were a part of the divine plan. Toil and effort, the painful winning of the daily bread from a reluctant soil, were only the later conditions imposed when sin had entered in.

Original man, morally and physically superior to his present condition, came into the universe as the invited guest of God to find a banquet prepared for him in nature's abundance, and the amazing spectacle of the cosmic theatre displayed before him for his admiration and delight. In Philo's scheme original man was created perfect. In Clement man was not perfect by creation, but created capable of attaining to perfection. Here Origen differs from his master; man was made perfect but fell through his abuse of freedom. All souls, with Origen, started in equality but differentiation came through freedom, the responsibility being entirely their own. For here there was a marked difference between the teaching of the Church and that of the Gnostics. The latter held that souls were born with different natures; some were spiritual, some hylic or material; between were the psychic or natural group, who could rise and fall, whereas a spiritual soul was spiritual always, and a material soul could never be anything else. But, it was replied, if nature is fixed, moral freedom is gone; the soul must then remain in its own condition and we are not responsible for our acts of choice. Moreover, Origen continued, it was plain matter of fact that character did change, the bad man became good, the good man bad. Thus when the soul enters into human conditions, its character is in no case so definitely determined as to leave it without moral freedom. Our salvation or election was not predetermined before our arrival here; it is of ourselves that we are thus or thus. The issue between what is due to nature and what is due to will is one which is frequently debated.

It may help us to understand the Alexandrine estimate of human nature if we notice the qualities they commend and the ways of life they deem most excellent. Reason is the sovereign element in man. The office of reason is to be a leader among the crowd of unreasoning faculties. It is the most lordly and most excellent element in our nature. It is the true man in the soul of each, the man within the man. The Stoic term, τὸ ἡγημονικόν, i.e. the ruling principle, somewhat difficult to translate satisfactorily, is freely adopted, and we find it in Philo and in Origen in many passages. It denotes the reason or self or personality or ego of a human being, and is sometimes said to be situated in the heart, because it is the centre of man's spiritual life as the heart is the centre of the body. It has often been pointed out that the psychology of the Alexandrines was not usually systematic. They inherited opinions from various schools and did not always unify all the elements they adopted. This is especially true of Clement, who has been accused of making undue use of manuals and collections. Still we may find a tendency where we cannot discover an articulate system, and a tendency most clearly evident in Origen is to regard reason or rationality as the highest factor in man's nature. It is not lost or suppressed for example by inspiration. Celsus had claimed for the Greek oracles that they were of more value and reliability than was generally admitted by the Christians. Origen's reply is to contrast the inspiration of the Pythian priestess with that of the Old Testament prophets. And the point of the comparison is that whereas the priestess passed out of conscious self-possession into a state of trance or ecstasy, so that her rational faculties were for the time in abeyance, the Jewish prophets received an illumination which did not extinguish but rather elevated the normal powers of the mind. It is the same view he takes when he deals with reason and revelation. All who have paid any attention to Origen's use of allegory have been struck by the strength of his conviction that in the Holy Scriptures the very treasures of divine truth are contained for our advantage. An inexhaustible wealth of spiritual knowledge is there for those who will penetrate beyond the letter. What is required is a true exegesis. And, little as we may be able to accept the strange results of Origen's allegory, its method in principle was strictly rational. The mind did not blindly accept God's revelation, after the manner of our latter-day fundamentalists. Rather to the interpretation of the given Scriptures it brought all the resources of reason and intelligence, discovering inner significance by a method valid then though no longer possible to-day. So the Logos or reason in man found and appropriated what the divine Logos or Word or Reason had embodied in the holy writings for our learning. The great Educator treated his pupils as intelligent beings. They were to seek to understand the mind of the Spirit, not to make surrender of their own.

And yet in this matter we cannot speak of the Alexandrines as holding one single view with unanimity. Some of them were definitely mystics, and mysticism is never merely a matter of the reason. Ecstasy, rapture, direct intercourse, the merging of the ego, are descriptions of a state in which we pass beyond the bounds of our normal consciousness into a higher communion. Origen never uses the term ecstasy, and probably never had the experience. Clement comes nearer to it in occasional phrases, but it is definitely found in Philo and is prominent of course in Plotinus. Philo speaks of inspiration as a condition which in some respects resembles intoxication. Some influence similar to that which caused the frenzy of Bacchic possession laid hold at such times of the soul and reason was no longer in control. He admonishes even his own soul to seek in ecstasy the good things of God. "Leave not only thy country (the body) and thy kindred (the outward sense) and thy father's house (that is speech or reason, *logos*) but also flee from thyself and depart out of thyself like the Corybantes." The mind in such a state of enthusiastic possession is no longer mistress of itself but is agitated and drawn heavenwards by the love of things divine. This is a spiritual emigration. The soul not only leaves the domain of sense but even abandons its familiar rational abode.

In Plotinus the highest stage of the soul's experience is contact with the Absolute, the One, the Good. It is an experience of the spirit rather than of the mind. It is a phase in which all other consciousness is lost in the sense of communion. An element of emotion is involved, so that, if we speak of it, terms of feeling are more appropriate than terms of thought. For it is in the nature of the absolute good to be the object of desire so that the soul in relation to it is drawn upon its upward way. This is the path which the musician and the born lover and the metaphysician follow, a path which lies through other countries than the straight austere road of reason. Much is said of love in this connection. The word Plotinus uses is the pagan ἔρως, which is a warmer term than the Christian ἀγαπή; it is spiritual passion but it is passion still, in spite of all the suspicion that gathered round the term πάθος. In its highest phase this experience leads us into the presence of God. We are united to that which we love. The isolation of personality is lost in communion. This is our advance to the topmost peak of the spiritual world, the goal of all our journeying. We are often reminded that our middle state is one of limitation, much as Philo remarked that Rachel went to the well with her pitcher and the pitcher would only hold a given quantity. But here we almost seem to be beyond our normal bounds of consciousness. Perhaps there may be a super-conscious as there is a sub-conscious state. There is a unity, a presence, a vision, higher than knowledge. These things the mystic has, not because he is a rational being, but because having reason he possesses also something higher. Inge says Origen and Plotinus had little to quarrel over and might have exchanged compliments. Perhaps on this one point they would have found agreement difficult, for Origen, as a French interpreter has pointed out, rigidly conserves spiritual personality. He knows nothing of any final absorption of the individual in the universal soul, and even in the momentary experiences of this present life individuality is not lost in communion. His mysticism did not carry him so far as that of Plotinus and to the end he probably regarded reason as the highest element in man's nature. But Plotinus could write; "In the vision of God that which sees is not reason, but something greater and prior to reason, something presupposed by reason, as in the object of vision. He then who sees himself when he sees will see himself as a simple being, will be united to himself as such, will feel himself become such. We ought not even to say that he will *see*, but that he will be that which he sees, if indeed it is possible any longer to distinguish seer and seen and not boldly to affirm that the two are one. In this state the seer does not imagine two things; he becomes another, he ceases to be himself and to belong to himself. He belongs to God and is one with him, like two concentric circles; they are one when they coincide, and are two only when they are separate. It is only in this sense that the soul is other than God. Therefore this vision is hard to describe. For how can one describe as other than oneself that which, when one saw it, seemed to be one with oneself?"

This high estimate placed on reason and by the Neoplatonists on mystic vision may be the explanation of the relatively slight importance which the Alexandrines attached to Faith. It is true that Clement speaks of it with some frequency. He describes it in Stoic phrases as a voluntary anticipation of truth, as the rational assent of an independent soul. He allows that faith is possible without learning, that it is the initial stage by which we pass on to knowledge and assurance. Both he and Origen were aware that many Christians were too easily content with faith alone, that when they had the worst of the argument with clever pagans they were only too ready to fall back upon the maxim: "Only believe." This had hampered and discredited Christianity with the educated, and Celsus was not slow to charge believers with indifference to serious enquiry and painful study in the quest of truth. Origen's answer is that if you plough a field or marry a wife or select a school of philosophy for your own, you act by faith just as much as the believer who comes over to Christianity. There is venture in all such commitals. Clement refuses to separate faith from knowledge. It is the earlier stage, but knowledge must complete what faith begins. Neither Origen nor Clement would accept the principle that salvation is by faith alone. The common charge against them is that they place excessive confidence in the power of intellect, reason, philosophy, to deliver us from evil.

Thus they restrict faith to the initial stages of religion, and we must remember that in their day the Creed was a baptismal formula and belonged to the entry upon the narrow way and not to the journey's end. The confidence of the Alexandrines in the higher faculties of human nature was indeed remarkable. The fathers might scold the Gnostics for their bold and unproved assertions, but they had indeed a Gnosis of their own. Their minds move among the verities of the spiritual world with an astonishing confidence, and beyond the range of evidence and demonstration it is upon vision and illumination, rather than upon faith, that they rely. We moderns have lost not a little of this assurance. Our oasis of scientific knowledge does indeed increase in area, but beyond it lie the uncharted, unexplored, immensities through which our thought can only move by faith. The large issues of God, Freedom, Immortality, are admittedly beyond our powers of determination.

"Nothing worthy proving can be proved." And a generation for which conviction has largely subsided to the level of hope may be conscious of an unwelcome contrast when it recalls an age in which the assured certainties of life seemed to be found at the top of the scale instead of at its lower end.

If it meant much to the Alexandrines that man was rational, it meant even more that he was free. Man's spiritual liberty was the cause of all his troubles, but also the condition of his greatness. For things are moved, they held, either from without or from within. What is moved from without, as you may move a stone or a log, undergoes an external compulsion, and is not in itself an agent. It moves or is moved without assent or action of its own. But the higher movement is from within, self-determined. An animal that moves from place to place has this capacity in a lower degree. Man has this power in its highest form. He can choose the good or the evil. "See I have set before thee this day life and good, and death and evil." Plato has said it as well as Moses; αἰτία ἑλομένου. Throughout the Alexandrine teaching, somewhat latent indeed in the Book of Wisdom, most fundamental and important in the scheme of Origen, there runs this doctrine of man's moral liberty. The only determinists were the Gnostics, and even they allowed freedom to the psychics, a middle class, who made their own future.

This freedom was taught and asserted rather than explained. Choice was free, but we exercise choice according to character, and how is character determined? By our own prior acts of choice. So you get a circle, if not vicious at least unsatisfactory, leaving the old riddle of freedom and necessity much where it always is. We must be content with noting the emphasis laid on freedom. Only the soul of man, said Philo, had received from God the power of voluntary movement, being in this regard made like unto God and liberated as far as possible—we note the limitation—from that stern mistress, necessity. With his divided nature, placed in a middle state between gods and brutes, man has the costly prerogative of choice, but the gain of freedom outweighs the loss. Clement especially, with his serene optimism, felt sure of this. It is the will of God that we should be saved of ourselves, by our own action. Only in proportion as we will them, do faith, wisdom and knowledge and even salvation become our own. Clement even takes over the Stoic theory that not moral choice only but even the mind's assent to the truth of a proposition is given by an act of will. Origen was more conscious than Clement of the burden and consequences of this responsibility.

Freedom is so closely connected with evil, he is so much more concerned to prove the righteousness of God than to assert the dignity of man, that in Origen's view the freedom, which he never questions, raises indeed many problems. But of its reality he has no doubt. Praise and blame and the discipline of God's punishments are inexplicable without it. He faces all the difficulties, the story of the potter and the clay, the hardening of Pharoah's heart, the vessels formed unto dishonour, all the passages which prove God's sovereignty rather than man's liberty, are faced, examined and explained, and if his explanations are not always convincing, his belief in human freedom is only the more evidently clear.

But if man is free and determines his destiny by his own acts, what meaning are we to give to such terms as Necessity, Grace, Salvation? In regard to Necessity there is difference of view among the interpreters of Plotinus. "He is without the least hesitation a determinist," says Mr. Whittaker. Dean Inge dissents, urging that Plotinus was convinced that mechanical necessity could not explain psychical or spiritual life. Caird agrees with the latter interpretation, which receives emphatic support from Zeller. Determinism indeed was hardly possible for a Platonist. If all is involuntary, Plotinus asks, what part is left for us? What of the

"We"? Where is there place for human agency? He is quite clear that human activity is not like the movement of a rolling stone, and that the planets do not compel us to virtue or to vice, and that even if bodily limitations constrain us we may work for our liberation with good hope to secure it. But it is also true that Plotinus is far more restrained than, for example, Origen in his assertion of man's freedom. Limits are recognized and not only those that are within. He considers the subject in a Tractate devoted to the discussion of Fate, and allows that environment is a cause as well as choice. He recognizes a sphere of necessity, a chain of events, a limitation involved by matter, the possibility of prediction and the place of Atropos the inflexible, and of Adrasteia the inevitable, in the world order. Man, he says, is a noble creation, yet only "as perfect as the scheme allows." In other words he believes in freedom, but it is a freedom within limits. We may not will the impossible, but we can will some things and, given this, the question becomes one not of principle but of degree. We remember that in Plato's *Timæus* the Cosmos had its origin in Reason and Necessity. The position of man, the microcosm, is similar; he is a being capable of purpose and subject to constraint.

Again, if man is free, what need has he of

grace? And if we are to be saved of ourselves, what occasion is there for a Saviour? Let it be said at once that grace does not mean for the Alexandrines all that it was to mean for Augustine, and that soteriology had not in their doctrinal scheme the place it filled with Marcion and St. Paul. In the main they love to discover harmony and orderly process rather than contrasts and strife. They were not men who had in their personal history experienced violent spiritual reactions. They had moved on, they had not turned sharp round. So when Clement invites his pagan hearers to salvation, what he has in mind is not deliverance from imminent peril of death but transition to a happier and better life. Habitually the Advent is represented as a momentous event, yet as one in a series, not the isolated intervention of God in a world whose condition was desperate, but a further and fuller stage in a gradual process which had gone on through many ages and would be continued in many more. It is not the strife, the antithesis, the warfare of the spirit the Alexandrines dwell on so much as the co-operation between God and man. It is by the courage of the defenders of the wall that God saves the city. It is by the labours of the husbandmen that God's bounty gives the abundant harvest. Sailors and pilot play their part in the storm, and so God brings the ship safe to port. From the same standpoint Plotinus regards providence as a power which harmonizes with human action. Man is within the cosmic order. He has his part in the drama, but he did not write the play. The individual soul never loses its relation with the soul of the universe. The soul that has descended will return to its own country because it wills so to do, and also because this is its ordained destiny. In all such views we lose the sense of opposition between the will of man and the grace of God, between the judge and the saviour, between purpose and environment. There is no minimizing of spiritual issues. There is no desire to abate the standard of spiritual attainment till it is within easy reach of the human grasp. The whole value of human freedom lies in the possibility of its use as a medium towards that likeness of God, ὁμοίωσις τῷ θεῷ, which is at once our destiny and our choice.

The Alexandrines were aristocratic in their estimate of human nature. Man at his best was their concern, but they had little regard for the crowd. The mixed multitude impedes the escape of the chosen people from bondage. It is a fit parallel to the indiscriminate mob of opinions which hinder the soul in its journey from bondage to the land where truth is found. Clement and Origen had to consider the rank and file of the Church, often uneducated persons, with strong convictions and little knowledge, ready to suspect any unfamiliar teaching and to attack whatever they did not understand as unorthodox. They are very patient with these believers of the simpler sort, the "simpliciores", the friends of the letter, to whom all culture and philosophy were suspect. But when Origen draws his distinction between the disciples and the multitude, when Philo says that the good are few and Plotinus sees in union with God the privilege of the spiritually élite, we are with the intellectuals in the lecture-room rather than with the crowds by the side of the lake. A philosophic multitude is an impossibility, Plato had said; and his followers believed him. They make great claims for man. He has reason. He has freedom. He has a divine element within him. But they are really thinking of the elect. Theoretically they might find fault with the Gnostics for their intellectual arrogance, but even Clement has little real sympathy with the average man.

This temper comes out in their depreciation of woman, for which perhaps we shall not blame them too much, as it was the habit of the period, and the Christian writers at any rate could shelter themselves behind the authority of St. Paul. Plato had said it was the penalty of the coward to be reincarnate as a woman. Philo said man represented reason, woman sense. Origen feared woman as a temptress, and was also irritated with women for chattering about domestic matters during his sermons. Women attended the lectures of Plotinus in great numbers, but he ignored them, much as Gautama did. We have a welcome instance of the truer estimate in Clement, who gives us a charming picture of the good wife, and provides a list of eminent women to justify his contention that woman is as capable of spiritual perfection as man. He speaks also of the higher femininity, $\dot{\eta}$ ἄνω θηλεῖα, a phrase which reminds us of Goethe's 'Ewig-Weibliche', the eternal feminine. The common attitude is to appreciate man at his best and to be quite silent in regard to the distinctive excellences of woman. It is aristocratic and to some extent ascetic. Celibacy was to become a virtue before long.

There is some interest in noting the types of human character and activity which the Alexandrines are ready to admire. The spiritual or contemplative life stands clearly above the life of action, but the latter cannot wholly be disregarded. So Plotinus allows that the virtues of the citizen, though they are unnecessary *There*, in the spiritual world, still have their value here and may help man towards the ideal. He has an interesting comment on Hercules, the pagan Saviour, as he appears in poetry. Because of his noble services Hercules is worthy of his place among the gods. But because his merit lay in action, not in contemplation, he is not wholly deified. A part of him, his shade, is still left in the lower world. The merit of service ranks below that of vision.

Philo gives a somewhat similar estimate of Joseph, the typical statesman. In the list of human ideals such a type is placed only in the fourth position. Abraham, the spiritual traveller, who migrates from the domain of the senses and of things seen to the Canaan of spiritual knowledge; Moses the prophet, the priest and man of God, are the types most praised. The statesman is inferior. Joseph's many-coloured coat denotes the mixed and manifold nature of political life. He was sold as a slave and the politician is in bondage to the mob. He was a dreamer of dreams, and what is life but a series of dreams that vanish, Shakespeare's "unsubstantial pageant"? The very chain of gold that Joseph wore when he rode as the honoured administrator in the second chariot might prove a chain of bondage as well as one of official dignity. The name Joseph means "addition", and Philo thought civilization was an addition to the laws of nature and right reason. So the recognition given to a life of great public service is not enthusiastic or generous. Joseph's ability, his competence in a time of national danger, his dignity and moderation in dealing with his brethren, his high personal character, are all allowed and even praised. But these were the virtues of the lower way, and when possible it was always better to keep aloof from public life. We remember the reluctance with which Philo had once been forced into it himself.

A second type, very different from the statesman and veritably Alexandrine in its main features, is the Christian Gnostic, as described by Clement. His appropriation of the term Gnostic from the heretics, and his claim that orthodoxy also could be enlightened, was bold and characteristic. The Gnostic has passed beyond the domain of mere faith. In his spiritual life he has vision and intelligence, so that his common acts are performed with full consciousness of their purpose, his prayers are uttered with understanding, his motives are ever nobler in quality than the mere fear of evil or hope of fame. Such a man after passing through stages of purification advances on the pathway of contemplative perfection and becomes the things he loves. His worship is not at stated hours but an abiding disposition. His prayer is not petition but an intercourse with God. He loves the highest and loves it for its own sake alone. His citizenship is in heaven, but he lives the heavenly life on earth. He has the help and guidance of God upon his ascending road, and when his spiritual advance passes beyond our power of description we know that, convoyed by the great High Priest, he has gone forward to indefectible blessedness, unbroken communion and final peace. Yet such a character is not inhuman and unapproachable, for he loves to do good, and will make use of this world's opportunities and even fill a public position if elected. He is always glad to teach what he knows to others, and in spare moments will read the Greek philosophers himself. Yet all this is by accommodation and not the Gnostic's primary interest. His real desire is to see God.

Two features in this character arrest rather than attract us. The first is Apathy, the superiority to feeling and desire, the freedom from liability to the influence either of pleasure or of pain. Clement took this over from the Stoics. The dread of the inward disturbance caused by emotion led these cold philosophers to eliminate it wholly from their ideal. The wise man and the Christian Gnostic after him must think and see and be united with his object, but passion, feeling, desire, must be overcome. It is a cold pure spirituality that remains. They did not know that emotion could be consecrated. Philo says that Abraham was entirely unmoved when he started out to sacrifice his son.

The other element which surprises a modern reader is the claim that the Gnostic could not only attain likeness to God, but be god, a god walking about in a human body. Divinization was common. The same age which made divinity absolute and unknowable made it also almost commonplace. The Greek and the Egyptian never separated God so widely from man as the Hebrew did, and so the Cæsars and the Ptolemies could become divine. "I said ye are gods," became a much-used text. A sort of apotheosis was possible for the Gnostic in this present world. We do not follow the Alexandrines here. In spite of such differences Clement's account of the higher life presents us with a noble and beautiful ideal. It belongs of course largely to its period.

We may notice, as a third type, Origen's conception of the Teacher's office. He took over the charge of the Catechetical School when he was seventeen years of age and remained a teacher till he died in his seventieth year. To few men has it been given to realize so fully in practice their own ideal. The nature of his career provided a combination of the contemplative and the active lives. He never lacked hearers and had a special attraction for the young, though it has been said that to

Origen himself the pressure of life's circumstances never allowed opportunity for youth. From his personal history and from what survives of his written work we can recover his high conception of what a teacher of men should be. The true teacher is a laborious student, living frugally, working long. He loves quiet, because it gives freedom for his task. His motive is the love of truth, never only the desire of affluence or popularity. He will instruct either the learned or the simple, adapting his teaching to their capacity. From the treasures of a stored mind he brings forth things new or old. He shuns and suspects seductive rhetoric and avoids the lazy repetition of truth grown stale and out of date. He is a bold enquirer yet reverent in his quest, believing it the will of God that man should continually learn. To him truth is welcome wherever it is found. He is conscious of his own limitations, asking the prayers and the forbearance of his hearers and suggesting views for consideration rather than asserting them as final truth. He is a man of catholic interests, as the following counsel given by Origen to his pupil Gregory may sufficiently make clear; "My desire has been," he writes in a letter, "that you should exercise all your natural ability in a constructive spirit, but with Christianity as your goal and aim. I would wish you therefore to take over from Greek Philosophy whatever studies can be made encyclic and preparatory to Christianity, and from geometry and astronomy whatever will prove useful for the interpretation of holy Scripture. I hope what the sons of the philosophers say about geometry, music, literary study, rhetoric, astronomy, that they are the handmaidens of philosophy, we also may say of philosophy itself in relation to Christianity." Such was the generous advice of a great teacher. It was in Alexandria that Origen had learned this wide outlook. He had formed his ideal in an ancient centre of learning, and it has outlived many that have proved less permanent. For ourselves to-day it retains its value.

It remains to ask what the Alexandrines thought about man's future. On the fundamental question of Immortality they were agreed. Man has a future. That "Our little life is rounded with a sleep" is the very negation of their strongest convictions. And they are greatly interested in the future of the soul. The assurance with which they discuss it contrasts strangely with the silence and hesitation which in some quarters prevail in our own day. We remember the teaching of the Book of Wisdom: "The souls of the righteous are in the hands of God." "Their hope is full of immortality." "The righteous live for ever, and the Lord is their reward." Philo treats the soul as in its very nature immortal. It is of divine origin, existing before the body and outlasting it. Clement and Origen are of the same mind. For the Gnostics too the soul descends and the soul returns. Plotinus is at pains to explain his dissent from the Stoic theory which made the soul corporeal. Essentially its nature is different from that of body; it is not generated and it may not be destroyed. So they faced the arguments of Epicureans and Sadducees without great concern. On certain points there were notable differences between the Christian and the philosophic doctrines, but on this main issue there is no dissent. The great "Perhaps" of Marcus Aurelius and of so many moderns did not trouble them.

Thus their theory of immortality is not conditional. Annihilation, which some of us are now inclined to welcome as an alternative to Eternal Punishment, has no place in any of the Alexandrine schemes. It is quite true that Philo speaks of eternal death awaiting the impious. But this death is not extinction. It is the unending endurance of suffering, the permanent loss of pleasure, desire and hope. The soul is so its own hell. The mark God set upon Cain was indelible. Here, as in the Gospels, we have the unforgivable sin. Something like this condition is supposed in Neoplatonism, when the soul descends from body to body, ever more and more involved in matter till at last it loses all strength to lift itself aloft again. It is heavily burdened, numbed into forgetfulness; it carries a great weight that bears it down. But it does not die. There is no extinction.

Neither again do the Alexandrines believe in any absorption. The individual is not lost in the universal soul. Each of us remains a separate self. This is especially clear in Origen. He foresees a long series of worlds but the soul in passing through them does not lose its personality. To the end it is a distinct hypostasis, and even when God shall be all in all individuality will remain. So there is no Nirvana; the spirit of Origen was too intimately Greek for such a final stage. Perhaps in the case of Plotinus the point is less clear. The individual soul in this life, though it does not lose its relation to the world-soul, is still a distinct and separate self, but the conditions of this life are not those of another. Inge writes: "It is not easy to answer the question how far individuality is maintained *Yonder*. For Plotinus unity is the source and highest character of true existence, separation, the very sign of imperfection and defect of reality." "Soul Yonder," Plotinus says, "is undifferentiated and undivided." The conclusion may be that in another world the distinctions which separate one soul from another are not lost but latent, so that persons are persons still but liberated from much which here is isolating and restrictive in personality. With this possible exception it may be said that the Alexandrines in their teaching on the life of the world to come retain a place for human individuality:

"Eternal form shall still divide
And I shall know him when we meet."

In Christian writers this belief is strengthened by the doctrine of the resurrection of the body. Philo knows nothing of any resurrection, and it has no place in the book of Wisdom. The Gnostics spiritualized the doctrine completely. Their resurrection did not involve the body. Plotinus was quite ready to allow many reincarnations, one life in the body after another. Death indeed is only a change of body. We go away earlier to come back sooner. We carry on into the next life the results of our actions in the life before. But it is always a fresh body, never a resuscitation of the old. The true resurrection is not that of the body but the soul's rising from the body altogether, when it passes, after many lives in many bodies, from the corporeal sphere and enters into the spiritual world. But of course for the Christian Platonists this purely philosophic position was not possible.

The belief in the Lord's resurrection had been too long an established article in the Church's creed for it to be abandoned. That the Lord did truly rise from the dead was final truth, like other items in the Apostolic teaching. Clement proposed to write a treatise on the Resurrection, but if he wrote one nothing of it has survived. The task was taken over by Origen; he wrote two books on the subject, and has in several other passages made his views clear. He was in a difficult position, liable to offend the orthodox, if he questioned the church's doctrine, liable to offend the educated if he defended the crude literalism of the simple believers.

He lays it down as a principle that, with the single exception of the Trinity, all rational beings need a body. They cannot live without one. This rules out the purely Platonic immortality. Origen is prepared to assert that such an immortality, suppose it were possible, has value, and that St. Paul's doctrine does not compel us to believe that a disembodied life must be necessarily worthless. But that is as far as Origen ventures to go. He retains the resurrection, but he boldly abandons the literal interpretation of it. He dwells on the nature of the body: it is in a condition of constant flux and change. The same material atoms may conceivably have belonged to more than one human body, and if there is to be a reassembling of such material at the resurrection, the difficulty is obvious. When the literalists asked, How then did the scriptures speak of the gnashing of teeth in another world? he retorted by a counter-question and asked them if souls in hell needed nourishment. The impossibility of this satisfied him that the teeth were figurative. So the body Origen retains is not this solid flesh but a more refined phase of substance, just as in the story of the Transfiguration the bodies of Jesus, Moses, Elias, were changed into an etherial radiance. The Stoics had a theory of seminal reason, a sort of germ-plasm, which without loss of continuity could assimilate other elements and transform them. Origen applies this to the doctrine of the resurrection. Individuality is not lost. Even physically we shall still be ourselves. Peter will still be recognizable as Peter, Paul as Paul. But we shall be changed. The nature of the risen body will correspond to the higher world in which man lives the risen life. The spiritual body is far more glorious than the natural body. It is devoid of weight. It is not subject to touch. He has in mind a highly rarefied almost gaseous condition of matter, something like Aristotle's *quinta essentia*, though he did not accept this additional element. So he saved the truth of the resurrection and looked for a future life in which the soul should not lack its appropriate habitation.

Such were to be the physical conditions, but the real interest lies in man's spiritual progress. Many ages, many worlds, had preceded this. Many would follow when this world had passed away. It is a tremendous vista. From phase to phase of being the soul moves on, still possessed of the dangerous gift of freedom whereby it falls or rises. Demons, even the devil himself, are capable of spiritual recovery, and the saint and the sage alike may fall again. It has been pointed out that so long as lapse and recovery are possible Origen's scheme has no more certainty of final attainment than the unprogressive cycles of Stoicism. It cannot be denied that in strict logic Origen's theory of a future, always doubtful because the will is always free, is difficult to reconcile with his final victory of good. In one place he suggests that the clash between freedom and final salvation will be reconciled through the power of love. If this be insufficient, we can only describe him as a universalist in spite of logic. The end, he maintains, shall be as the beginning. The original perfection of humanity, as it existed in the mind and purpose of God, lost through the fall of souls and the abuse of freedom, will eventually be regained. The endowment so reappropriated will be veritably our own, for we shall have recovered it by our acts of choice. Through pains and penalties, through the wise and purifying fire, through many reincarnations, man is destined to pass to a state of final unity, when the last enemy shall be destroyed and God shall be all in all. Nothing worth saving has been lost. Nothing alien survives to mar the harmony. In much of his teaching Origen shows a troubled mind and lacks the serenity of Clement. But in his final universalism he is boldly optimistic. "As it was in the beginning." There is complete restoration. Plotinus, differing in many respects from Origen and always less interested than the Christian teacher in man and his destiny, gives fundamental assent to Origen's position when he says that, however numerous the intervening stages, there is correspondence between the beginning and the end.

In the universe, as the Alexandrines conceived it, what is the place of man? How is he related to the world he finds around him? How shall he discover affinity and harmony between what is without and what is within? And can we with any good result compare the Alexandrine answers to these large questions with the ideas of our modern world? What contrasts or correspondences can we discover between ancient philosophy and modern science? If Sir James Jeans will on occasion quote the *Timaeus* of Plato, how much does it imply? One or two points of contact between the old and the new it may be worth while in concluding these lectures to suggest.

Man had affinity, so the ancients thought, with the highest forces of the cosmic order. Mind, reason, spirit were dominant in the universe and were also discoverable in man. Even the unnameable Absolute was as near to him as to any other created being. What was There or Yonder in the spirit-world was also Here in the life of man. So the microcosm reproduced the macrocosm. The divine Word by whom all things were made had his seat also in human personality. The individual soul never lost its relation to the world-soul. Between the world of Being and of that of Becoming there were links and avenues. If man's place in the spiritual scale was not the highest, if angels, æons, stars, principalities, powers and departed souls in bliss seemed to surpass him and outshine him in their vaster glory, still he was of their company, claiming kinship and affinity with the highest of them. He belonged to the universe, was at home therein, could believe that it was friendly, was assured of his place in the unity that lay beyond its seeming discord.

The moderns too have had much to say on man's kinship with the universe. But what has mainly occupied them has been his physical relationships. Man's place in nature has been assigned to him by Darwin, Huxley and their followers, and to-day we all allow his evolution from lower to higher forms of life. The old world thought about man's spiritual descent; the soul came down. We think of his physical ascent, and indeed it is a wonderful story. Interest centres on man's upward development. He may possess all the spiritual qualities the ancients attributed to him, nay he does possess them. But it is his physical affinities that have occupied us of late. His kinship with nature is much in our minds. And in the universe as we know it and interpret it his higher nature does not find its affinities so evident as they were of old. Love and moral purpose and the spiritual values are not for us written large upon the universe as they seemed to be in the days of Origen and Plotinus. The macrocosm does not reassert the highest elements of the microcosm. It was Huxley himself who told us in his Romanes Lecture that in the highest issues man's business was not to live according to nature but to fight against it. "The ethical progress of society depends not on imitating the cosmic process but in combating it." The science of to-day is not of course exactly that of Huxley's Lecture in 1893. Time may restore what the Victorians missed. But for the present we have not the clear vision the Alexandrines had of a spiritual world, a κόσμος νοητός, in which all man's highest values had their origin and guarantee.

Perhaps a second contrast may be discerned in the character of man's hope for the future. The Alexandrine outlook was definitely individualistic and other-worldly. The real good for man was to "fly hence", and attain to spiritual communion in another world. Just as Plato cared only to be a citizen in the heavenly city, so the eyes of his followers were set upon a higher state of being, where stage after stage the soul might pass into indefectible blessedness. It was an individualistic ideal, the solitary flight of "the alone to the alone", the mystic union of the soul with God.

A few in our modern western world, a few people whose value is out of all proportion to their number, still look towards the future with this great spiritual hope. But the majority of good men and women are leaving life's great open questions to be solved when life is done, and are meanwhile aware that the human race may have ten billion years still to spend on this planet. Mankind, we are told, is still very young. The "Juventus Mundi" did not close with Homer. If man has done much in a short time, what may he not accomplish before a heat death, "in which the total energy of the universe is uniformly distributed and all the substance of the universe is at the same temperature", brings the cosmic story to its close? Democracy, science, rapid and easy transport, closer international association, are all tending to the solidarity of the race, and our future hopes take a corresponding tone. The individual is counting for less and less. We have the mass movement for the great man, the action of society in place of personal responsibility. And we look forward, at best, to a possible kingdom of God on earth, at the lowest, to a slight rise in the mediocrity of average human nature. But the ideal to-day is collective, social, corporate, mundane. Some of us find it very inadequate. Others make noble sacrifices for a better world which they will not themselves behold. Let us, in any case, not forget the sympathy of Jesus for the multitudes in Galilee. But Galilee was not Alexandria.

It has been said that there was something dramatic in the cosmology of the ancients. The story of the universe began, proceeded in successive acts, and reached its term. The descent and eventual return of the soul had a similar character. The many worlds of the Stoic theory were a series of minor dramas. The Christian scheme of salvation was admirably adapted to be represented as a mystery play. The author of the drama, God, Reason, Nature, unless it was Fate, saw the end from the beginning, and man being rational could understand the plot and see the relationships of the characters and the sequence of the scenes. And the whole might prove a success, even if some characters were villains. But what baffles us in modern science is the absence of any ultimate purpose which we can recognize and approve. It is not only that the immensities at times humiliate and oppress us, not only that we find ourselves dwarfed and withered by the vastness of space and the onward sweep of the multitudinous years, it is the blank inability to find in the whole process any evidence of a worthy objective, that leaves us as silent and frustrated as Job was when the Lord spoke to him out of the whirlwind. "I sent my soul through the invisible"; and the soul wanders to and fro, like Noah's dove, finding no rest. All this activity, radiation, atoms, waves, stars, electrons, extra-galactic nebulæ, wonderful, stupendous, ineffably magnificent—but why; for what end? The ancients were not mistaken in calling it a cosmos. It is an order, not a chaos. "He bringeth out their hosts by numbers; not one is lacking." The ancient dislike of the unformed and the indeterminate is justified by the precision of nature's ways as now we know them. The moderns agree with the men of old on the wonder and order of the universe. But the ancients thought they knew what it all meant and frankly we do not. We have no latter-day equivalent for the great dénoument of the cosmic drama as Origen sees it: "God shall be all in all." So we watch the play without understanding the plot. The dramatic unities may not be those with which we are familiar; we have no hint or suspicion as to how the story is going to end. Perhaps there will not be any end, just a fading out, a dying sun, no consummation, no term or boundary of being in which the spirit of man can rest content.

In these ultimate matters we are of course out of our depth, beyond our range. Let us come back from speculation to reality and see whether there is anything to justify our reappropriation of the assurance and optimism of the Alexandrines. We are told to keep our religion and our science distinct, but such a severance is quite impossible. It is said that thirty years ago we thought we were heading towards an ultimate reality of a mechanical kind, whereas to-day the stream of knowledge seems moving towards a reality which is at any rate non-mechanical. Attention has been naturally arrested by this change of outlook on the part of science. No sane apologist for the cause of the angels will wish to count probabilities as assured results and to be guilty of premature exultation at the supposed reconciliation of science and religion.

But from the standpoint of the idealist and the believer it is definitely notable that the constitution of the universe is asserted to be intelligible through mathematics and therefore rational, that the abstract and therefore restricted and partial character of the older science is allowed, that the place and function of the mind in the fabric of knowledge and of being is recognized. We are passing into a different climate of opinion. How far this process may advance, what further place may be discovered in a material world for spiritual values, no man yet may say. Crude matter, of which the ancients thought so poorly, may yet admit of a higher interpretation. After a long circuit, by methods of a widely different character, more restricted by experiment and less confident in speculation, we may yet be brought to an estimate of the universe in which nothing of real value in the Alexandrine outlook has been irrevocably lost.

INDEX

This Index is mainly one of Names. The Subjects with which the Lectures deal will be found in the Table of Contents.

Abraham, 58, 61
Alexander, 12, 16
Alexandria, 10, 12, 16, 18
Ammonius Saccas, 11, 35
Appian, 19
Apollonius of Tyana, 36
Arabs, The, 10
Archimedes, 13
Aristotle, 15, 16, 75, 94, 104, 111, 119, 172
Arius, 10, 71
Athanasius, 10
Augustine, 81, 158
Aurelius, M., 93, 113, 168

Basilides, 11, 37, 50, 137
Bevan, Ed., 95
Bigg, C., 131
Brahmins, The, 36
Buddhism, 136

Caesarea, 11
Caird, Ed., 35, 77, 156
Celsus, 29, 121, 144, 147, 152
Chaeremon, 93
Cherubim, The, 58
Chrysostom, Dio, 13
Clement, 10 and often
Cleopatra, 12
Copernicus, 104

De Faye, E., 51, 65, 120
Demetrius, Bishop, 11
Demetrius of Phalerum, 16

De Principiis, Origen's, 26, 72
Dicaearchia, 12
Dionysius, 93
Drummond, J., 101, 136

Eddington, Prof. A. S., 84, 103
Empiricus, Sextus, 17
Epicurus, Epicureans, 36, 98, 119, 168
Eratosthenes, 103
Ethics, Aristotle's, 134
Euclid, 17

Florilegia, 16

Galen, 134
Genesis, Book of, 21 and often
Gnostics, Gnosticism, 11 and often
Goethe, 161
Gordian, Emperor, 35
Gregory, 166

Harnack, A., 31
Heraclitus, 129
Hercules, 96, 161
Herod, 142
Herophilus, 17
Hipparchus, 104
Homer, 17, 177
Huxley, T. H., 134, 176

Inge, W. R., 35, 151, 156, 169

Jahwe, 24, 37
Jeans, Sir J., 84, 85, 106, 174
Jeremiah, 15, 142
Job, 47, 97, 106, 121, 142, 179
Joseph, 162
Joshua, 19

Lucretius, 118

Magi, The, 113
Marcion, 43, 50, 61, 98, 158
Maximus of Tyre, 73, 132
Mead, G. R. S., 35
Mithra, 125
Moses, 15, 66, 108, 154, 172
Museum, The, 10, 17, 131

Neoplatonism, 16 and often
Nirvana, 169

Origen, 10 and often

Pantaenus, 30
Paul, St., 48, 98, 106, 108, 110, 117, 123, 134, 158, 160, 171, 172
Paedagogus, Clement's, 66, 124
Peripatetics, The, 17, 119
Peter, 114, 172
Phaedrus, Plato's, 126
Pharaoh, 142
Pharos, The, 12, 38
Philo, 10 and often
Photius, 101
Plato, Platonism, 14 and often
Plotinus, 11 and often
Porphyry, 35
Psalms, The, 24, 126, 133
Ptolemies, The, 10, 12, 15, 16, 38, 165

Ptolemy, Cl., astronomer, 104
Pythagoras, 84, 90, 104, 105
Pythian Priestess, 147

Republic, Plato's, 90
Rome, 11, 50, 83, 93, 113

Sarah, 60
Satan, The, 47
School, The Catechetical, 11, 30, 165
Seneca, 93
Serapis, Serapeum, 12, 15
Socrates, 73, 96, 121
Sophia, 52, 98
Stoics, Stoicism, 27, 29, 92, 108, 115, 119, 121, 124, 140, 146, 152, 155, 164, 172, 178
Strabo, 13
Stromateis, Clement's, 29

Tertullian, 65, 113
Timaeus, Plato's, 18, 22, 29, 42, 90, 101, 115, 123, 157, 175

Valentinus, 11, 50, 98, 104
Virgil, 117

Whittaker, T., 156
Whitehead, Prof., A. N., 84
Wisdom, Book of, 10, 17, 70, 119, 137, 154, 167, 170
Williams, Prof. N. P., 81
Word, Hymn to the, 68
Wordsworth, 132, 141

Zeller, Ed., 45, 156

For Product Safety Concerns and Information please contact our EU representative GPSR@taylorandfrancis.com
Taylor & Francis Verlag GmbH, Kaufingerstraße 24, 80331 München, Germany

www.ingramcontent.com/pod-product-compliance
Lightning Source LLC
Chambersburg PA
CBHW061448300426
44114CB00014B/1888